I0442159

Copyright © 2016 Randa Lee Roberts

ISBN 10: 1532842708
ISBN 13: 9781532842702

www.randaleeroberts.com

DEDICATION

This book is dedicated to my children, Shelby and Sawyer, who are my greatest blessings in life and my reason for striving to be the best person that I can be at all times. As your mother I grew in ways that I couldn't have imagined. I learned how to love, trust and support unconditionally, and how to help others through guidance while providing encouragement to individuals seeking to find themselves and their own way.

To all of the wonderful children whose lives I was able to influence, teach and inspire as an educator who in return inspired me to embrace every opportunity to give it my all.

To my amazing parents who were both young and inexperienced but taught me what being a family truly meant through the constant love, devotion and never-wavering attempts to better themselves in an effort to provide only the best for me and my siblings.

It is because of all of these people and the beautiful smiles, sweet hugs, undeniable love and support that have made my life the most wonderful and fulfilling experience a person could ever imagine.

TABLE OF CONTENTS

ACKNOWLEDGMENTS

It is because of the amazing opportunities that I have been given over the years working alongside parents, their children, other educators and administrators that I am able to share with others my insight into so many topics which involve children, the learning process and life experiences. I hope that individuals who are involved in the lives of children in any capacity can utilize the information, strategies and tools of the trade to make each experience both meaningful and rewarding for everyone.

Shelby C. Williamson, Sawyer M. Williamson, Dorothy Lee McPherson, my father, the late, Joseph Gordon Roberts, my siblings Teresa Kay Roberts (Todd), Annah Rebecca Roberts (Jiminez), Kathryn Morgan Roberts, and my fiance' Robert A. Hammond. The University of Florida, Florida State University, University of West Georgia, Okeechobee County School System (South Elementary School), Leon County School System (Hartsfield Elementary and Kate Sullivan Elementary), DeKalb County School System (Main Street Elementary), and Coweta County School System (Canongate Elementary and East Gate Elementary Schools).

INTRODUCTION

Ever since I can remember I've desired to teach others, whether it is with my younger siblings, friends from the neighborhood, or simply while playing make-believe. This has been the underlying basis of many of the things I've done throughout my lifetime.

When I was a young adult it became clearer that this desire to instruct or teach would become a permanent part of my being. While a college student, I began teaching physical fitness and toning to individuals employed within the State of Florida's many agencies around Tallahassee. I coached youth soccer at the YMCA, while also working and teaching dance at a local health spa. My desire to teach was innate.

As an adult, I was honored to teach over 500 hundred young students during my tenure in the classroom. In addition, I taught college interns to become exceptional classroom teachers before leaving the profession to focus upon raising my two children.

After working within the school systems in Florida and Georgia, I continued to maintain my education so that one day I may step back into the classroom. Life, however, had other plans for me and my career. I decided to work as a teacher in different capacities over the years including training mothers how to run a successful business from home while raising their children. This ultimately proved to be a wonderful way to share my love of both children and families while making it possible for mothers to provide an income. The benefit was allowing mothers a chance to remain at home with their children to actively engage and teach them every day. A lot of parents only dream of doing this while their children are young.

In 2009, I continued my desire to help families, teachers, caregivers and children through sharing information relevant to children through my parenting website, Childrentopics.com. It is my hope that you can use many of the tips and suggestions outlined in detail within the pages of this book series so that raising your child can be as rewarding to you as raising my children was to me.

CHAPTER ONE

WHAT BEGINS WITH THE LETTER "A"?

Teaching Children Accountability

"It's not my fault!"...

The famous last words that I know each one of us have heard at one point in time. In fact, we've probably used the phrase ourselves even knowing that the statement couldn't be further from the truth.

It seems that a lot of children growing up in the current generation believe that they don't have to be responsible for their words, actions or failure to act. Consequences for their choices are nothing more than an afterthought. As parents, teachers and caregivers, *it is our responsibility to teach children that they must be accountable* for the decisions made. By teaching accountability early in life, we will ensure an easier transition into adulthood.

Children should not be an exception from being held accountable in their daily lives. If we simply excuse their poor choices without holding them accountable, we are reinforcing the behavior we are trying to prevent. In addition, we are enabling the inappropriate choices or behavior and **encouraging** the child to duplicate the poor choice in the future. Parents and teachers should utilize these moments as "teachable moments". Use the opportunity to discuss "why" the decision or action was inappropriate, "what" should have been done instead, and "how" the consequence(s) of their words, action or behavior will impact them or someone else ("who"). By utilizing teachable moments we can **raise** our children to be people of character.

Teaching our children accountability is fundamental to a child's growth and development. It is necessary as it affects how they deal with persons of authority, relate to their siblings and associate with peers. Without these fundamentals, children may transition into adulthood without understanding that they, too, must be accountable for their actions. Unfortunately, the likelihood of the penalty being more severe is probable as the child ages.

Everyday life experiences provide the perfect setting for teaching children accountability and consequence as they relate to the decisions they make. Here are a few suggestions or tips:

- **Assignment of Chores:** One of the first steps in teaching accountability could be assigning your child age-appropriate chores to complete either daily or weekly. For younger children it might be wise to establish a schedule that is posted in a visible location with the days of the week and the chore on the day it is assigned. This will allow a method for your child to review and check-off completed chores. Prior to your child completing the chores, make certain that he/she is aware of the reward(s) for completing the chores as well as any consequences that you deem appropriate should the chores not be completed as scheduled. It is your responsibility to verify that the chore is completed satisfactorily and to provide the reward specified. If, however, the chore has not been completed, you will need to hold the child accountable by enforcing the consequence. *(NOTE: If you fail to follow through in either reward(s) or consequences,* **you** *aren't being accountable).*

- **Involve your Children in Extracurricular Activities:** Most children are already involved in some form of extracurricular activity whether it is a sports team, dance, scouting or youth group. Children will often pressure their parents into signing up for an activity because someone they know is involved or because it sounds "cool" only to discover that they aren't really interested in it and they want to "drop out". WAIT!!! Teaching your child that he/she committed to an activity which 1) had a fee involved; 2) involve other people who are counting on him/her is mandatory to teaching accountability. By establishing the importance of following through until the activity ends, teaches a valuable life lesson and holds them accountable to their decision.

- **Examine Feelings & Emotions:** It is human nature to allow feelings and emotions to guide our thoughts sometimes **resulting** in impulse decisions. Teaching critical thinking skills will help your child process their feelings and emotions before making important decisions. It is wise to review situations, such as outlined in "teachable moments" above to help your child learn how to get his/her feelings and emotions under control in order to tackle the decision with a clear mind. An example of this would be the child that is being bullied to dive into the river under the bridge that he must walk across on his/her way home. The child knows there could be **serious** danger in doing so but, he/she wants to be accepted by his/her peers. A child who reacts without thinking may simply dive right into the water beneath becoming injured. A child who has been taught to control his/her emotions and think about the consequences of his/her actions may choose to walk away from the taunting avoiding injury.

- **Never Give Up!:** As frustrating as it may be to remind your child for the one-hundredth time to do something, parents, teachers or caregivers should NEVER give up. It is our job to teach our children to be accountable for their words and actions. If we give up, they will not learn. Eventually persistence will pay off. Be consistent. As it is stated in Proverbs 22:6 (NIV), "Train a child in the way he should go. When he is old, he will not turn away from it."

Now that we've addressed a few tips to help teach your children accountability, let me quickly review some points of reference when teaching your children. You might even post them in a conspicuous place to remind him/her:

Always:

- Do what you're supposed to do.
- Persevere.
- Do your best in everything you do pursuing excellence.
- Show that you demonstrate self-control and self-discipline.
- Think before you act.

Never:

- Blame others for your words, actions or mistakes.
- Give up.
- Disappoint those who are counting on you (unless it is immoral or illegal)

Remember, a person of character is one who is responsible, diligent and accountable. A person of character always considers the consequences of his/her actions before making a decision to act. As parents, it is our responsibility to teach our children character traits. Take every opportunity as "teachable moments" arise and provide the fundamentals necessary in the growth and development of your child.

The "Not-So" Basics of ADHD & What Parents Can Do to Help!

Who knew there was such a thing as Attention-Deficit/Hyperactivity Disorder and when did it suddenly come about? Has it been around since our grandparents were children, or did it only appear in the last 20 years?

Answer: It has been around for nearly half a century in the United States first being referenced in the 1970's (http://www.ncbi.nlm.nih.gov/pmc/articles/PMC1525089/).

It seems that every child and some adults too, at some point(s) in time are naturally wound up whether from excitement of an upcoming event, too much soda or snacks containing sugar or perhaps one too many cups of coffee. However, after the "moment" wears off they are capable of functioning normally. Whatever the reasons, for some children (and adults) the inability to focus or concentrate on tasks at hand makes everyday life and living frustrating and difficult, especially when it is an everyday occurrence.

There are different *types of* Attention Deficit/Hyperactivity Disorder (**ADHD**) including:

1. **combined ADHD**, which is the most common type, and involves all of the symptoms (which will be outlined below)

2. **Inattentive ADHD**, formerly known as ADD (Attention Deficit Disorder) which is indicative of impaired attention and concentration.

3. **Hyperactive-impulsive ADHD**, which is associated with hyperactivity without inattentiveness.

ADHD is common in both young children and teenagers; however adults can also suffer from the disorder. Typically, when an adult is diagnosed there will be variations found in their symptoms. Adults may experience restlessness instead of hyperactivity and are often known to have consistent difficulties within their interpersonal relationships and employment throughout their lifetime. The disorder is also more common in males than in females.

As an educator, parent, and former coach I've seen many children in my lifetime and enjoyed the presence of every one of them although some more challenging than others. It seems that I cannot go anywhere without coming into contact with a child or adult who has been diagnosed with ADD or ADHD, or who has questions regarding the disorder and options available for the treatment or reduction of the symptoms. Interestingly enough, many of the individuals with ADHD appear to function just as normally as those without the disorder(s). Many individuals, especially children, suffered immeasurably and found it difficult to make it through the most basic and simple tasks. This couldn't have been more evident than in the classroom.

As a teacher of elementary aged children, I had the opportunity to teach over 500 children during my years in the classroom. Although teachers aren't allowed to diagnose a child whom they believe may have symptoms relating to one of the disorders above, they are the individuals who have the greatest exposure to the child during the course of a day, while engaged in activities or with their peers for the duration of the school year. In fact, documentation that teachers supply must be relied upon for doctors to make their diagnosis as the visit with the child may last 20 minutes. Teachers probably have the MOST hands-on experience in handling children with the disorder, implementing tools and strategies to help these children manage themselves and helping them learn how to engage with others in a productive manner.

Let's look at the main symptoms of ADHD:

- Difficulty paying attention to details; carelessness; making *mistakes* in school and other activities; producing messy and often illegible work.

- Easily distracted by nominal stimuli; *frequently* interrupting their work and that of others to tend to irrelevant noises or events that most others can ignore.

- Inability to pay attention or remain on task; or to focus on activities in which they're engaged.

- Frequently unable to finish schoolwork or tasks that require concentration.

- Frequent shifts from one activity to another without completion of anything.

- Procrastination.

- Disorganization not just in their tasks or work habits but in their surroundings.

- *Forgetfulness* in daily activities, assignments and tasks. Often these individuals will miss appointments, deadlines, forget to bring lunch or lunch money, etc...

- Will often ignore or "forget" the rules of engagement in activities in social settings.

Hyperactivity will present additional symptoms which are noticeable in preschoolers and nearly all young children before the age of seven. These symptoms will include:

- Squirming when seated (or expected to sit) and fidgeting;

- The need to get up and walk around the room regularly.

- Young children will express the need to run or climb excessively even during inappropriate times; whereas teens may appear restless.

- Inability to play quietly or to engage in quiet leisure activities.

- Always on the go!!!

- Excessive talking and it doesn't even have to be "to" another individual but aloud to themselves.

Impulsivity, another symptom associated with ADHD will often be classified as a demonstration of the following behaviors:

- Impatience - cannot wait his/her turn; instead of walking in line behind the leader, he/she will often break out into a run and pass the line and leader;

- Difficulty delaying responses - child will not wait for the teacher to finish a question before blurting out an answer (even if the answer is completely off-track);

- Constantly interrupting others or inviting him or her into social circles where he/she may not be desired often resulting in problems within the social or work setting.

- Engaging or initiating in conversation(s) at inappropriate times and places.

- "Clumsy" behaviors frequently leading to accidents such as knocking things over or running into people or objects.

- The tendency to engage in dangerous activities without first thinking about the consequences of their actions.

There are many treatments available for children with ADHD depending upon the nature and severity of the symptoms that the individual experiences, the Doctor's recommended treatment plan and the parents willingness to take the necessary steps in managing many factors.

Treatments for ADHD:

- Behavior Therapy/Behavior Management

- Dietary Modification & Management

- Medication

As with most disorders, there are a variety of treatment options available. Let's discuss Behavioral Treatment(s) for those suffering with ADHD which, along with dietary modification & management, are MY recommended first treatment choices.

Behavior Therapy/Behavior Management for treating ADHD:

The implementation of a behavioral therapy program is based upon the principle that children want to behave in socially acceptable ways. The assumption is that children want to please their parents and feel good about. Secondly, children enjoy receiving positive consequences for their behavior which is obvious when a child beams with delight over receiving a special reward or privilege. Finally, most children behave appropriately to avoid negative consequences such as those typically following unacceptable behavior(s).

Behavior therapists or therapy increases the frequency of desirable behaviors by increasing the child's interest in pleasing their parents and by the provision of positive consequences when the child behaves in the desired manner. To counterbalance this program, therapists consistently provide negative consequences every time an inappropriate behavior occurs. Although basic in description, this is the philosophy behind behavior therapy.

1. The first step in behavioral treatment therapy is to improve or enhance the positive feelings between parent and child. Usually this can be accomplished by setting aside time each day for "special time" between the parent and child. During the designated time, there should be "no" outside interruptions such as work, telephone calls, etc...And should be devoted exclusively to the child and having a positive experience with him/her. Usually, the child dictates the activity that will take place. Remaining positive through both your words and actions will increase the positive interaction. By showing and demonstrating your undivided interest in your child and what he/she is doing, feeling, etc....you are allowing your child to reciprocate those feelings by wanting to please you too. Parents who've engaged consistently in this type of "special time" or "child centered activity" will find that their children will respond more positively in many situations including completion of chores, homework and independent responsibilities of the child.

2. Part two and the second focus of behavioral treatment involves positive consequences for behaving in appropriate ways. When your child does or is doing something that you want to encourage more often you should comment on it. Praise goes a long way with young children. This part is up to the parents and/or teacher. Make it your goal to recognize your child at a minimum of 5 times per day doing something that you'd like to increase the frequency of him/her doing. The result is that children will recognize their parents noticing and

appreciating their efforts at behaving well and the desire to do so will increase too. An example of positive reinforcement using acknowledgement would be a statement like, "Thank you for carefully walking down the stairs."

In order to make behavior therapy successful, it must be consistent and relevant to both the child and parent. Designing an effective program should include the following:

- Providing both a clear and concise description about the behavior that is expected of the child in order to earn a reward is necessary in order for the child to process and practice. For instance, "clean up your toys" is vague and may not be understood by the child whereas; "pick up your toys and put them in your closet on the shelf" is much more conclusive about your expectation.

- Establish reasonable expectations for the child to avoid setting the child up for failure. An example of an unreasonable expectation might be requiring a 4 year old to scrape the leftovers from his/her plate into the garbage can after meal time. This expectation would be better suited for a child 10 years old who has better fine motor skills, etc...

- Determine a realistic number of areas with which you intend to focus. In other words, don't try to correct every single problem area that your child has at one time as this will be overwhelming and unproductive. Choose a few of the most important "problem areas" and devote your time and attention only to those until you see the desired behaviors consistently being practiced.

- Involve your child in choosing the types of rewards he/she will receive. It is understood that if a child is genuinely interested in the reward(s) and system in place, he/she will be more inclined to accomplish the established goal.

- Initial success is imperative to the plans continued success. Always design a program that will allow the child to enjoy success in an effort to motivate them to continue striving to reach the established goals or desired behaviors. Modifying the criterion as time moves forward is reasonable.

- Social rewards are equally as important as tangible rewards. Praise, aka social rewards, are something that everyone, even adults, respond positively too. By increasing your use of praise, as long as it is genuine, the positive relationship between you and your child will continue to increase as well.

- Consistency. I cannot express this enough. In order to be successful you have to apply these techniques in a consistent manner. Every day, every success or infraction must be met with the rewards or consequences set in place.

Negative Consequences to Reduce Misbehavior:

Just as important as positive rewards and reinforcement is the consistent implementation of negative consequences. In utilizing behavioral treatment plans, you must enforce negative consequences and/or punishment in order to reduce the frequency of undesirable behavior. First you must ensure that the child understands "what" the undesirable behavior is in order for him/her to correct or modify it. For example, the behavior that you are targeting in an effort to eliminate is "talking back".

1. Ensure you provide examples of "back talk" that you consider inappropriate and unacceptable.

2. Although you want to eliminate unacceptable methods of responding, you don't want your child to feel unable to express him/herself in a positive way. Teaching the child acceptable ways to disagree with you is your goal.

3. Review the rewards your child will earn if he/she is able to communicate appropriately without the use of "back talk".

4. Identify the consequences or privileges the child will lose if he/she engages in inappropriate forms of "talking back".

By providing your child with clear and concise examples, rewards and consequences you are teaching your child that there is simply no positive related to bad or inappropriate behavior.

Now that we've reviewed a few of the behavioral techniques that are effective in teaching children with ADHD more appropriate ways to behave, let's focus on another important factor in helping children who suffer with the disorder.

Dietary Modification / Management:

This is truly an area that more emphasis should be placed by parents and not just on children suffering from ADHD. All parents should consider the foods they are feeding their children. In the research and studies conducted of dietary effects on children with ADHD it was noted that there are a variety of considerations every parent should review and implement. If parents can assist in controlling their child's behavior with simple dietary modifications vs. medication, it would seem the only clear and reasonable choice.

Studies indicate that the foods that we eat, or don't eat, have a dramatic effect on children with ADHD. In fact, for some children, dietary modifications alone can serve as an effective treatment. Diets that are lacking in essential fatty acids and amino acids have been linked as a contributing factor for children suffering with ADD and learning deficiencies.

Taking a closer look at a child's diet and making a few careful modifications, we might be able to reduce the symptoms associated with the disorder and perhaps replace or eliminate the need for pharmaceuticals with a healthier diet.

A few dietary points to consider:

- Children who ate a meal high in protein performed equally as well in school, and sometimes better, than non-hyperactive children.
- Children who consumed essential fatty acids within their diets showed significant improvement in terms of a reduction in their symptoms.
- Although not all children suffering with ADHD show nutritional deficits of the essential fatty acids, a significant number of children do lack this nutrient.
- Fatty acids stimulate both brain and nerve tissue in the body and are critical for proper growth, mental function and the development of the immune system. Our bodies do not produce the two critical fatty acids, Omega 3 or Omega 6 which are key elements in the *reduction of ADD and ADHD* requiring that we ingest them as a part of our daily nutrition.
- Omega 6, which is more common in our diets than Omega 3, is delivered through corn, sunflower, canola and safflower oil, margarine, vegetable oil and shortening.
- Most Americans, young and old, are deficient in the fatty acids delivered through Omega 3. The impact on males is more substantial as they require higher levels of this fatty acid than others.

Foods rich in Omega 3's:

- Flaxseeds ****
- Walnuts
- Salmon

- Chinook
- Sardines
- Soybeans (Cooked)
- Halibut (baked/broiled)
- Shrimp (steamed/boiled)
- Tofu (raw)
- Snapper (baked/broiled)
- Scallops (baked/broiled)

By including these foods within your diet daily and/or weekly, you will provide your child the essential fatty acid that has been linked, along with Omega 6, in reducing the symptoms associated with ADHD.

Note: Flax seed and flax oil are the richest plant source of Omega 3 fatty acids and offers Attention Deficit Disorder nutrition vital to support healthy childhood behavioral and IQ development. It is recommended that children (and adults) with ADHD consume approximately 2 Tablespoons of Flax oil daily.

Here are some simple suggestions in how you can incorporate flax seeds or oil into your daily dietary regimen:

- Mix 1 tablespoon of flax oil in flavored yogurt or ice cream.
- Add 1 tablespoon of flax oil in fruit smoothies (use ice to make it more like a milkshake.
- Mix 1 tablespoon of flax oil with one tablespoon of maple syrup or honey as a sweetener for drinks or baking instead of using granulated sugar.
- Use 1 - 2 tablespoons of flax oil when preparing tuna or egg salad decreasing the amount of mayonnaise that you'd normally use.
- Flax Butter - Melt one stick of organic butter and mix with 4 ounces of flax oil. Pour into a container that you can refrigerate and use in place of margarine.
- Omega 3 Ice Cream: Mix 2 cups of yogurt with 1 tablespoon flax oil and fresh or frozen fruit. Serve when frozen.

Note: Using flax as a dietary supplement for the treatment of ADHD symptoms will require continued use as it takes approximately 10 - 12 weeks for the elevated levels to be recognized in brain cells. Don't give up prior to the benefits actually having the time to become effective.

Additional dietary considerations should be made when attempting to reduce the symptoms associated with ADHD. Below are a few other dietary points to ponder if they are implemented.

- The inclusion of other amino acids into the diet is necessary when addressing ADD and ADHD nutrition. Amino acids, from which protein is made, are essential for the child suffering with either disorder. By its inclusion in the diet, ADD & ADHD people have shown a significant reduction in the level of unfocused or misdirected energy demonstrated throughout their day. Getting back to basics - it's that simple!
- Start the day with a solid protein based breakfast - out with the sugary cereals, pancakes slathered in syrup, sweet rolls or doughnuts, instead try the following:

    o   Scrambled or boiled eggs, toast w/flax margarine & fresh fruit
    o   Whole wheat toast w/flax margarine or peanut butter
    o   Fruit and yogurt smoothie (following recipe above)
    o   Protein shake
    o   Bacon and eggs w/toast (flax margarine) and milk
    o   Egg and sausage patty on English muffin
    o   Yogurt (with flax seed oil)

- **Foods to avoid feeding your children with ADD or ADHD include the following**:

    o   If it's wrapped in cellophane, don't feed it!
    o   A diluted fruit juice, i.e. 1 small glass of apple juice contains the sugar equivalent to 8 apples.
    o   No NutraSweet! (Or other artificial sweeteners).
    o   No processed meats and NO MSG! If the ingredients contain words you can barely pronounce as a part of the contents, don't feed it.
    o   Avoid foods & snacks that contain food coloring especially red & yellow.
    o   Cut back on sugar consumption.
    o   Eliminate foods that contain additives such as aspartame and nitrates.

- o Although some studies indicate that the consumption of caffeine has improved symptoms, it is recommended that your child not consume items containing the ingredient as the side effects of caffeine outweigh the benefits.
- o Eat fewer simple carbohydrates such as candy, corn syrup (or foods containing it), honey, sugar, products made from white flour, white rice and potatoes without the skin.
- o Focus on a diet rich in complex carbohydrates such as fruits and vegetables most notably oranges, tangerines, kiwi, grapefruit, pears and apples as these will also aid in a good night's rest.

There are a few additional dietary areas which you might want to review and consider altering should your child suffer with ADHD. These elements are often missing from a child's diet and result in nutritional deficiencies. The majority of Americans don't meet the Recommended Dietary Allowance (RDA) for magnesium, including children. Several studies show that ADHD children are deficient in many common minerals, most often in magnesium, zinc, and iron, and that magnesium supplementation significantly decreases the hyperactivity symptoms in these children. Why are so many diets lacking these important minerals? Processed ingredients and foods!

- 99% of the magnesium in sugar cane is lost when it is refined to white sugar.
- 80 - 96% of magnesium content in wheat is removed when refined to white flour.
- Consumption of soft drinks (pop or soda) decreases the body's absorption of magnesium.
- The typical high-dairy, high fat North American diet contains almost four times as much calcium as magnesium. This unbalanced ration coupled with the high fat content tends to suppress magnesium absorption.
- Further, high levels of dietary or supplementary calcium tend to suppress magnesium absorption.
- Refined salt is practically void of magnesium.

With this knowledge, why not switch to whole wheat flour, sea salt, and use natural sweeteners like Stevia, molasses, agave, and dried fruit in place of sugar? The processed foods are one of the main causes of most any disease in the modern world as they've replaced the wholesome, mineral and amino rich ingredients that we once used in our kitchens!

The final area that we will review is the treatment of ADD and ADHD using pharmaceutical   drugs.

Medication as a Form of Treatment:

Modifying and maintaining a child's diet seems impossible, especially if the child is a picky eater. Some families are far too busy or simply don't see the results to the level or degree that medication can offer. Determining which medication their child will be administered to treat the symptoms of ADD or ADHD is a big decision.

There is a wide variety of medications on the market used for the ***treatment of ADD & ADHD.*** ADHD has been attributed to a dopamine deficiency in the brain. So, you might be asking, what does dopamine do for us?

The chemical dopamine plays a vital role in the way the brain controls our movements. Not enough dopamine, a child will experience very little movement or the ability to control his/her movements well. A brain with too much dopamine results in uncontrollable subconscious movements like picking, tapping, repetitive moments, jerking, twitching. Dopamine also controls the flow of information from other areas of the brain, and regulates memory, attention and problem-solving tasks. When dopamine is released it provides feelings of enjoyment and reinforces us or motivates us to do, or continue doing, certain activities. Dopamine is released by naturally rewarding experiences such as the enjoyment of good food, laughter, pleasurable experiences, etc... This pre-programmed reward system makes sure that people eat, and do other things that make us happy which helps us to survive. Without enough dopamine, people feel the opposite of enjoyment and motivation -- they feel fatigued and depressed, and experience a lack of drive and motivation.

Pharmaceuticals, such as Ritalin, Ritalin SR or other amphetamines increase dopaminergic activity which decreases hyperactivity and stereotypy which is the extent of variation in a behavior under a given set of conditions.

For parents choosing to go the pharmaceutical route, according to the American Academy of Pediatrics, it is likely that at least 80% of the children taking stimulants will respond, so if

1 or 2 medications don't work or have unwanted side effects, then a third might be tried.

Stimulants such as Ritalin, Concerta, Focalin, Metadate CD and Adderrall, are considered to be among the first line of treatments available, with antidepressants considered the second line of treatments if 2 or 3 stimulant medications don't work for the child. Stimulants include different formulations of methylphenidate and amphetamine available in short, intermediate and long acting forms.

Making the decision "which" medicine to try will depend on many factors including the doctor's recommendation, the medicine most often used for treating specific symptoms that your child demonstrates as well as the age, weight and capabilities of your child. For example, the decision of which medicine your child will take will be a little easier to make if your child can't swallow pills. While there are no liquid formulas of any of the stimulants, the short acting ones, such as Ritalin and Adderall can usually be crushed or chewed if necessary. The sustained release pills must be swallowed whole (except for Adderall XR).

Even though medicines have their place in the ***treatment of ADD and ADHD***, no medication is free of side effects. Those common of stimulants can include a decreased appetite, headaches, stomachaches, trouble getting to sleep, the jitters, and social withdrawal. Many of these side effects can be managed by adjusting the dosage or modifying the time when the medication is administered.

For parents that don't want to administer stimulant medications to their child, another option is available. Strattera is the main non-stimulant medication that is approved to treat children with ADHD. Although not used as commonly as stimulants, such as Vyvanse, Focalin XR, or Concerta, Strattera does have a place for kids who don't tolerate stimulants because of side effects or because stimulants just don't seem to work for them.

Long-Term Prognosis for Individuals Suffering from ADHD:

Approximately 20 to 30% of children who suffer from ADHD will develop learning problems that may not improve with treatment. Implementation of some form of treatment as well as resources to assist you in teaching learning strategies to compensate are available through outreach programs and within most school systems. Some of these children, those with hyperactive behavior may develop other disruptive disorders such as conduct and oppositional-defiant disorder. The reason for the association is still unknown.

Many children with ADHD will learn to adjust and function with minimal residual effects. Unfortunately, those who show symptoms of conduct and oppositional-defiant disorder are more likely to drop out of school and find it difficult to thrive in their careers later in life.

Impulsivity and hyperactivity tend to diminish with age, inattention and the inability to focus and finish tasks is something that can persist through adolescence and into adulthood.

Final Thoughts:

Denying that your child has symptoms outside of the normal characteristics demonstrated by children his/her age or making excuses for continued behaviors is not in the best interest of your child.

By allowing inappropriate behaviors to persist and continue without intervention, the more difficult they will be to change. It is critical for parents to stop the escalation of misbehavior typical of children with ADD and ADHD by seeking professional help and implementing the strategies available.

Whether you choose to utilize the Behavioral Strategies provided above, focus on the necessary and recommended dietary modifications outlined, or even administer prescription medicines to your child (or perhaps a combination of all of the treatments suggested) it is in your best interest and that of your child to DO SOMETHING!!! By choosing to ignore or pretend that there isn't a problem, you are ultimately allowing your child to suffer immeasurably which may result in many unthinkable outcomes.

It is recommended that you seek the attention of a professional if you feel that your child demonstrates unhealthy levels of any of the symptoms provided. The sooner you seek professional support for your child the better.

Assertive Discipline in the Classroom

Assertive discipline is a structured, systematic approach to discipline that is extremely effective to educators along with other tools of the trade in running an organized, teacher-in-charge classroom environment. Often, it seems, teachers have a difficult time managing or unable to control undesirable behavior(s) from occurring in their classrooms. Part of this can be attributed to a greater frequency of ill-mannered students lacking the basic concept of respecting other people and their property, but can also be attributed to teachers who are weak in areas of behavior management. Assertive discipline has evolved over the years and is more or less a combination of an authoritarian discipline approach with a tendency toward more democratic and cooperative elements.

The underlying philosophy of assertive discipline is that a teacher deserves the right to teach her students without anyone preventing her from teaching or without anyone preventing another student from learning. It encompasses a teacher's right to decide what is best for the students within her classroom and to establish rules and guidelines to assist in attaining the goals and expectations established. Through the effective implementation of assertive discipline including student compliance in creating and maintaining an efficient learning environment, teachers can attain the academic goals established by handling discipline problems and disruptions assertively instead of aggressively.

When using assertive discipline in the classroom, there are a few basic criteria in order to make its use effective. For instance:

- A few clearly stated classroom rules (posted & reviewed regularly).
- A teacher's ability to immediately and confidently react when a situation presents itself requiring behavior management.
- Providing firm, clear and concise directions to students in need of redirection/focus.

Additionally, much the same with any effective behavior management plan are effective techniques necessary for any level of compliance and success:

- Reinforcement of appropriate behavior(s) by complying students.
- Negative consequences imposed on students disobeying rules and directions.

When utilizing assertive discipline in the classroom, teachers must control their impulses to use abrasive, sarcastic or hostile comments. Students are not a teacher adversary. Additionally, teachers must avoid reacting in a passive, inconsistent, timid or non-directive manner. Children are able to determine the strong vs. weak and will take advantage of and conquer those not capable of taking charge.

Rules and boundaries set by parents establish the base for security and learning to behave in both acceptable and appropriate ways. Students arrive at school expecting the same of their teachers. It is a teacher's responsibility to establish the rules and boundaries that students must operate within and without a clear and concise plan, a teacher will be unsuccessful in managing her classroom.

Teachers implementing assertive discipline are more than just directors of their classrooms. They must establish and build positive, trusting relationships with their students and are responsible for teaching appropriate classroom behaviors utilizing various methods in which to effectively communicate the expectations set in place. For instance, simply telling a classroom full of students might reach 2 out of 24 students, but what about the remaining 22? Teachers need to "teach" students appropriate classroom behaviors through not just direct instruction but through the following as well:

1. **Describing expectations.** Some children require a "painted picture" in their minds in order to clearly understand the information being shared. Using examples and non-examples allow students to clearly envision what is expected of them.

2. **Modeling rules, routines and expectations.** Not only must you use words to describe the behaviors which you would like your children to adhere, modeling (role play) is another valuable tool to ensure clear delivery. Involving the students in modeling is a wonderful method for teaching children to internalize the information disseminated - especially utilizing students that have more difficulty adhering to the established rules and routines.

3. **Practicing & reviewing expectations.** Teachers should provide opportunities for students to simply practice the rules and lessons taught as they relate to behavior management. During the first week of school, I provided many opportunities teaching my students what was expected of them. I found that allowing the extra time in the beginning stages of the school year my students were able to internalize

my established routines and behaviors. This resulted in every week being more rewarding for all of us. By occasionally reviewing the rules & expectations, I was able to "nip" inappropriate behaviors before they got out of control.

4. **Encouraging words vs. condescending words.** In all of the years in the classroom and raising my children, I've found that "honey" is sweeter than "vinegar" when it rolls off the tongue. Students respond to your requests, rules and demands 9 times out of 10 when encouraged in a positive manner. One student I taught had earned a reputation for being a little unruly and difficult to manage. I paid careful attention to his interactions my first day with my classroom and found that he didn't respond well to negatives. Sure, he'd eventually stop the misbehavior, however not until after making a scene, disrupting others and becoming so upset that he was unable to regain focus. The second day, knowing his triggers and what areas he found particularly difficult in which to conform, I offered him kindness, as well as a "class responsibility" as line leader encouraging him to set a good example for his classmates by following the rules of the classroom. Almost immediately his attitude changed. We had a pleasant, positive day in which he earned, for the first time the entire year, a small treat for excellent behavior(s) and attitude.

5. **Rewarding efforts and attitudes.** People of all ages enjoy the rewards of following established rules and guidelines and for putting forth the effort needed to do so. Children especially enjoy rewards for their efforts to follow rules, live within the boundaries established and for demonstrating a positive attitude. Children will make mistakes. However, they also will do things that are exceptional and recognizable through words of praise, encouragement and even a simple reward at times. It might be something as little as earning some candy for walking down the hall quietly; perhaps five extra minutes of recess or free-time; or even a big shiny star on the behavior chart. Whatever the reward, children will be grateful and elated to have been recognized for their efforts. After all, everything tastes better with praise!

Assertive discipline works most effectively if you adhere to the following techniques:

- Never fall victim to the belief that there is any acceptable reason for misbehavior (unless biologically based misbehavior)

- Establish four to five rules that you'll implement within your classroom. Post them in a clearly visible location.

- Determine negative consequences for failure to follow the rules. You'll want to choose three to six negative consequences in order to have a "discipline hierarchy" in order to effectively manage and correct repeated misbehavior. Remember, you'll enforce consequences EVERY time a student misbehaves. (NOTE: The first course of action when teaching appropriate and inappropriate behaviors is to "talk" to the student. Often times, simply conversing with the student about his/her behavior and your expected behaviors will correct the behavior without the need for extreme penalty.

- Create positive consequences for appropriate behaviors. There are many types of positive(s) that a teacher should use daily in the classroom including verbal praise, stickers; special "leadership" roles i.e. line leader, caboose, lunchroom monitor, etc. The sky is the limit and an area that most teachers have very little difficulty in creating. Including "Group Rewards" is also a wonderful method for encouraging the desired behaviors you expect within your classroom. This not only encourages individual students but reinforces positive behaviors amongst your students as they encourage one another to behave appropriately. Group rewards might include a special Friday snack, recess at an out-of-the ordinary time or even a movie.

- Class meetings are an effective method for teaching your rules, expectations, routines, boundaries, rewards and consequences. Children need to be aware of "how" the program is going to work in order for it to work and be successful.

- Include your students in 1) establishing the rules; 2) recording them (age appropriate) and taking them home to be signed by their parents. Parents should also be aware of your disciplinary style and classroom management program in order for it to be effective.

- Begin your program immediately. Never allow a day to pass without rules, rewards and consequences being in place.

- Practice assertive discipline daily and techniques that lead to its success:

Express your displeasure with the student's behavior (not the student) and then explain what the child should have done instead. Providing examples of correct behaviors are necessary to encourage the child to practice what you desire.

Immediate recognition of appropriate behaviors is necessary if you want them to continue. By focusing only on the negatives at the expense of failing to note the positives, you'll end up dealing with more negatives. Keep in mind that some children may become embarrassed when praised or disciplined so remember to practice both verbal and non-verbal forms of both.

Repeat, repeat, repeat! *To be effective you'll need to repeat your commands and/or rules repeatedly until they are internalized by your students and can be followed. My husband tells me I sound like a broken record which is exactly what it is, "broken record" technique. What he doesn't realize is that he does the same thing at work with his employees who are all adults??? An example:*

Teacher: "Sara, you need to complete your math. Please return to your seat.
Student: "But I want to see the bird on the fence."
Teacher: "I understand but you need to complete your math now."
Student: "Just one minute, OK?"
Teacher: "No Sara, I want you to return to your seat now and finish your math."
Student: "Augh! Okay!"

- Learn "positive repetitions" technique. When using this technique you are repeating your rules in an effort to reinforce them to all students. This is accomplished by using positive statements to students that are demonstrating the desired behavior(s) e.g. "Ben raised his hand to answer the question." "Thank you for raising your hand so that I could call upon you for a turn."
- Proximity praise is another technique of assertive discipline. This is used instead of always focusing on the misbehaving child or children and is quite effective at redirecting the misbehaving child. For instance, "Thank you Maddie, Sean and Jacob for cleaning up your center areas so that we can go outside for recess."
- Another technique is proximity control which includes moving toward the misbehaving students. Typically a misbehaving child will notice your impending presence and will refocus and/or redirect his attention to what it is supposed to be upon. **Note:** For older students, an invitation into the hallway to talk privately will often prevent embarrassment in front of peers and will allow for you to successfully deal with the disruption or misbehavior.
- Teach, Practice, And Repeat! Teachers must teach their students the desired classroom behaviors if they still don't have them after repeated attempts of redirecting, rewards and consequences.

Effective classroom management is the responsibility of the teacher. In order to be successful it must be consistently implemented without variation. Students must be taught the rules and boundaries within which they are expected to function. A well-administered discipline plan with incentives in the form of rewards and positive reinforcements save time so that the purpose of being within the classroom can be effective. If a teacher is "too busy" to teach the rules and then enforce them consistently, he or she will be forever out of time.

CHAPTER TWO

WHAT BEGINS WITH THE LETTER "B"?

Banishing Blemishes

There is probably nothing quite as aggravating as the occasional pimple that shows up just in time for that special outing or event. Talk about timing! And as many times as we've been told "not" to squeeze, touch, or tamper with them, we just can't keep our hands off of it. After all is said and done, we realize that the advice we chose to ignore was actually the best advice of all.

Whether you're a teenager, pre-teen, or adult, pimples seem to make their way into our lives especially when juggling life's demands. The good news is that most adolescents outgrow acne. The bad news is that half of all adults have acne in some form or another. Why? Unfortunately with so much environmental pollution and toxins, medications of one type or another and hormone injected meats and dairy products, it's no wonder we see an occasional breakout. But besides all of these elements is the dreaded "S" word - STRESS!

With life as hectic as it can be, it's no wonder that we don't have hair falling out by the handfuls on top of the pimple that may rear its ugly head on our cheek, forehead, chin or worse, our nose! In women, who seem to be more prone than men in getting pimples, it can be related to hormonal changes, more oil production in the skin than ever before, certain types of birth-control, and even pregnancy or menopause. Pimples, or acne, can also be the result of treatments that were used during adolescence such as benzoyl peroxide, or Retin-A. Regardless of what causes us to have those blemishes, there is something that you can do to help treat and perhaps eliminate their occurrence.

There are many topical treatments available at the local drugstore, retail, or department stores. The problem is, with so many to choose from, which do you choose? Some treatments that you can use are less expensive, very effective, and extremely convenient since most of the ingredients are something that you probably already have at home.

Topical Treatments:

Acne prone skin is something that should be treated gently. In fact, washing one's face twice a day should help to resolve most problems that may arise. When washing the face, you'll want to massage it gently as opposed to scrubbing it with harsh chemicals or even pressure. Choose moisturizing products that are oil-free and non-comedogenic certain that you exercise the same restraint when choosing makeup.

Let's check out some wonderful methods to clarify and treat the skin like royalty.

- *Steam:* Steam has long been used to open the breathing passages when someone is congested and prefers NOT to use medications. The same is true when it comes to opening the pores to release the blockages that eventually become pimples or the help to eliminate oil and dead skin cells that can lead to pimples as well. Simply boil water, add a handful of strawberry leaves, eucalyptus, thyme and/or wintergreen, place a towel over your head to trap the steam and lean over the bowl or pot for 10 to 15 minutes. NOTE: Remove the pot from the burner BEFORE leaning over it with a towel.

- *Natural Clay Mask:* Clay is a phenomenal way to open pores but make certain that you are using the right kind. Art clay is NOT the right choice; neither is digging clay out of your yard. Combine a tablespoon of Kaolin clay or Fuller's Earth with rose water to form a paste; spread it over your face leaving it on for *approximately* 10 minutes. Rinse with tepid (warm) water.

- *Tea Tree Oil:* One of my all-time favorites as this ingredient can be used for so many things. Known to be a strong anti-microbial, it fights the enemy that can contribute to pimples. You'll simply apply a 15% solution to the blemishes twice a day. Make certain that you **do not** apply it to broken skin as it will sting if you do.

- *Calendula:* This ingredient is also a wonderful anti-microbial and anti-inflammatory which is perfect for healing damaged skin. Simply apply the herbal ointment or a tea directly to the blemish and you'll notice a difference in no time.

- *Aloe Vera Gel:* Another ingredient that most households should have "on call" containing anti-bacterial, anti-inflammatory and astringent properties. What does all of this mean? It means that it is a pore-minimizer. Simply apply it to the skin after washing your face and allow it to do the rest.

- **Baking Soda:** Simply add water to baking soda and create a paste (similar in thickness to that of toothpaste.) Apply to the blemish by rubbing in a circular motion. Allow it to dry. You may leave the transparent mixture on and apply make-up or remove it to apply.

Now I'm sure you've heard the phrase, "feed your face" well here's another take on the phrase which actually suggests that there are certain things that we want to eat that acts as "food for the face." In other words, diet may actually contribute to acne so you'll want to monitor your food consumption to help eliminate ingredients that actually seem to contribute to your acne.

Feed Your Face:

- **Complex Carbohydrates:** Eating complex carbohydrates may actually be something that will help. Carbohydrates that have a high (GI) glycemic index such as sugar (sucrose, fructose, corn syrup); processed and refined foods; white rice and bread; pasta and baked goods made with white flour) are digested really fast resulting in the blood sugar (glucose) and insulin levels to spike. According to some studies, this may actually influence the development and severity of acne. On the contrary, a diet high in protein and low GI (complex carbohydrates) such as whole-grain products including breads, cereals, brown rice; beans, lentils and split peas; and fresh fruits and vegetables seemed to help reduce breakouts.

- **Omega-3's:** In the case of inflammatory acne, a severe form of acne, research suggests that consuming Omega-3's will help by suppressing inflammation throughout the body. You'll obtain the most Omega-3's by choosing cold-water oily fish such as salmon and sardines; flax seeds; and Omega-3 supplements if necessary.

- **Supplement Your Skin:** As mentioned, certain environmental toxins may wreak havoc on the complexion. By supplementing your skin, you'll be able to combat acne by detoxifying the liver, fighting bacteria, regulating male and female hormones, and reduce inflammation all at the same time. Remember, women produce both types of hormones which trigger enormous levels of oil production. These items are available at many natural food stores. If you're pregnant or considering getting pregnant, please talk to your doctor before taking any of the natural herbal supplements.

Milk Thistle: This comes in a standardized extract. You'll want to take 200 milligrams, three times per day for best results.

Burdock (tincture): Sixty drops, three times per day.

Bupleurum (decoction**): Use 15 grams bupleurum and 5 grams licorice adding it to water or juice. Drink approximately 2/3 cup, three times a day of this mixture.

Goldenseal (tincture): Sixty drops, three times per day.

Dandelion root (decoction**): Drink 1/2 cup, three times per day.

Green Tea: Drink 1 cup 10 minutes before each meal.

Vitex (chaste tree), saw palmetto and gentian: Speak to an herbalist regarding quantities.

** - Cover 20 grams of the chopped dried herb in 3 cups of cold water, bringing it to a boil, then allow it to simmer for 20 - 30 minutes until the liquid is reduced by one-third. Strain the herb and store in a cool place. Drink this liquid either hot or cold.

As with any acne treatment or application, you may not see immediate results and consistency is the key. Taking care of your skin, the largest organ in the body, the same way that you take care of your heart is imperative to overall good health. To improve the look, texture, and glow of your skin, you'll want to make certain that you replicate the process every day for optimum results.

Teaching Children How to Handle Bullies

Not too long ago, a young boy was found "hanged" inside his closet. His suicide was attributed to having been bullied to the point that he could stand it no longer. Sadly, his parents, teachers and classmates didn't realize the severity of the pain and suffering this young boy endured on a daily basis. Even more disappointing is the fact that the boy had been told to "toughen up" and not be such a wimp.

Bullying is a BIG deal. In fact, if simply ignored it can lead to serious problems or have serious results such as the event outlined above. The results of a recent query of students at the elementary school level suggested that approximately three-quarters of the students questioned indicated that they'd been bullied or teased to some degree. When asked what type of bullying they'd endured, they shared stories of being called hurtful names, teased, threatened, kicked, hit, pushed around and even forced to do things that they didn't want to do. When asked how bullying made them feel, the replies were unanimous. It made them feel hurt, scared, sick, lonely, embarrassed and most of all, sad.

Bullying is most common at the elementary school level (especially in second grade), followed by junior high (middle school) and then at the high school level. It is estimated that a shocking twenty percent of all American school children have been the victim of some form of bullying during elementary school. What's more shocking is that the same percentage admitted to having "bullied" someone as well.

What is Bullying?
Bully is the intentional, purposeful tormenting of an individual(s) in physical, verbal or psychological ways. Bullies attempt to take advantage of others whom they perceive as weak. The use of verbal and physical aggression is typically the means for achieving their goal of "mental control" over and submission of the victim. Bullying doesn't just bother the victim though. It bothers everyone and can make school, the playground or even the bus ride or walk home from school a place or situation that creates fear instead of a "safe" place in which to learn and/or play.

Why do people Bully?
Bullying is done for many reasons; however the most typical reason it seems is to feel adequate in the presence of their peers, most likely to cover up their own feelings of

inadequacy. Research suggests that bullies have difficulty making friends. Through the act of bullying others they gain a certain level of popularity, a false level of respect and peer status among their classmates. Bullies tend to be rejected by and disliked by many of their classmates. They are lacking in social skills, always tend to be in conflict, behave more aggressively than their peers and typically engage in immature play.

There are reasons for bullying which may include poor parental role models, children coming from homes which can be characterized as cold, lacking warmth and affection and with poor familial relationships. Bullies typically lack self-esteem, struggle with a severe jealousy of others and struggle academically. This is not to say that some bullies aren't your typical average child. Sometimes bullies can be well adjusted children, who've for whatever reason, fallen in with the wrong peer group leading to acts of bullying.

Which Characteristics do Victims of bullying exhibit?

Victims, at the elementary level can be male or female as bullies don't discriminate. In middle school and high school levels, bullies are more likely to be boys picking on other boys of the same age and can be grouped as both bullies and victims. This is not to say that girls don't participate in bullying because they do. They are more inclined to verbally harass someone than to physically attack their victims (although it has occurred).

Victims are typically children who are considered to be social isolates or outcasts, those demonstrating poor social skills, physically or emotionally weak and those perceived by others as "different". But it doesn't stop there. Victims can include children who are in the wrong place at the wrong time (for the victim) but the right time for the perpetrator. Bullies also target sensitive children because a great deal of the thrill of bullying comes from watching the reaction of the victim.

Symptoms of Victimization:

More often than not, victims of bullying do not confide in or report incidences of abuse to school officials or their parents, much the same as rape victims and physically abused children and adults. Why? Typically, failure to notify someone about being victimized is due to additional threats of abuse by the perpetrator. Some children are embarrassed that they've fallen prey to another individual. While others fear that telling someone will result in interventions by parents or teachers that will make the tormenting worse. Therefore, mums the word! It is because of the bullies emotional stronghold over the victim that parents and teachers alike need to be sensitive to and able to detect alterations in a child's emotional, social, physical and academic status. There are many characteristics identifiable in children who've become the victim of bullying. Below are just a few:

- Almost out of nowhere, children who once enjoyed going to school express a sudden dislike of school. In fact, it is not uncommon for the bullied child to begin missing school suffering from unexplained illnesses due to the fear of being bullied.
- Children who once engaged happily in family activities become moody, sullen and avoid family interaction.
- Loss of appetite, except when they get home from school when they appear to be starving, and difficulty going to sleep.
- Waiting until after school and safely at home to go to the bathroom.
- Loss of interest in schoolwork, sports, extra-curricular activities and a drop in grades.
- Disheveled appearance upon return home from school, including but not limited to torn, stretched out or stained clothing or unexplained cuts & bruises.
- Requests for extra lunch money or allowance, school supplies, etc....
- Behaves depressed.

What Can Parents Do?

Teaching our children *how to handle bullies* is necessary just like teaching them how to brush and floss their teeth. They don't enter the world equipped to handle being bullied.

- If you notice your child is behaving differently than normal, it might be a good idea to engage in meaningful conversation to determine what is troubling your child. Remember, your child may be withholding relevant information so you'll have to assess the situation to the best of your ability. By creating a safe environment for your child in which to feel comfortable, he/she may be more inclined to share this type of information. If you've maintained an "open door of communication" with your child, it might benefit him/her in sharing details of abuse he/she is suffering at the hands of a bully. If you suspect your child is being victimized, but won't open up about the situation, you can begin a conversation by establishing a scenario such as, "I dropped by the school today to drop off ____and noticed a young boy in the office very upset. It seems he was being bullied. Has this ever happened to you? This might encourage your child to share his/her situation with you.

- Expressing your feelings or perhaps sharing your own stories of being bullied may put your child at ease and reduce his/her fears that you'll blame him/her for being bullied. For whatever reason, children fear that you'll consider their situation their fault. It is imperative that you help your child understand that being bullied is not their fault but the fault of the perpetrator.

- Explaining the personality characteristics frequently shared by bullies will be helpful in your child's ability to comprehend "why" he/she is being bullied. It removes the blame from your child's mind and places it where it rightfully should be placed. And, although we don't really want to "blame" anyone for bullying, it might help your child understand and also allow them to breathe a much needed sigh of relief.

- *Teaching your child strategies on "Dealing with Bullies"* is very important, in fact, it could be the most important thing you can do in the prevention of future episodes. And although the elimination of bullying altogether might take a few days, or a couple of weeks etc....at least your child will be better equipped.

Strategies to Improve Your Child's Self-confidence Thereby Reducing Vulnerability:

1. First, teach your child how to *avoid being an easy target*. Focus on image related issues such as maintaining a strong, upright posture; practice along with your child using a firm tone of voice while maintaining eye contact. Explain how slumping the shoulders and looking away from the bully will only make you appear vulnerable. The few "image makeovers" alone will speak volumes about your child's new level of self-confidence vs the old level of vulnerability. Practice in a mirror or even videotape your child so that he/she can review the images and see just how he/she is being portrayed to others. It is also a good example for you to allow your child to videotape you as well while demonstrating these skills.

2. Suggest that your child avoid isolated areas which prevent him/her being seen by others. Bullies tend to "bully" when they feel that they aren't in a position to get caught by an authority figure. This is especially true in the bathroom, on the playground or even when walking home from school or the bus stop. Your child should always be aware of his/her surroundings and those individuals "looking for trouble".

3. Teaching and re-affirming within your child the positive attributes that he/she possess' is an important part of re-establishing his/her self-esteem. Another way of doing this is by slowly building your child's social network and teaching

"socialization skills". Being a parent you may not feel that anything is wrong with your child's social skills or demonstration of those skills, but there is something leading to the bullying. Having spent thirteen years in the classroom, primarily in second grade, I had many parents who were insulted when their children were bullied and the child's lack of social interaction with others was addressed. Parents have to swallow their pride and focus on what is best for the child. Perhaps inviting a classmate or two over to spend time with your child so that he/she can establish meaningful & positive relationships that will carry over into the school environment will begin the healing process at school. Additionally, parents establishing relationships and a social network with other parents from your child's class will prove beneficial in your child's efforts to heal, as well as your own wounds, by creating a community of adults who will have your child and their own child's best interests in mind. (No parent likes a bully).

4. *Role playing with your child can be a very effective strategy in teaching your child "ahead of time" what can be done in order to avoid situations that include bullies.* By teaching him/her NOT to obey the commands and/or demands of the bully through the use of a firm voice while maintaining eye contact your child will not only improve his/her self-confidence but be able to know what to do when a situation presents itself without being caught off guard. I recommend instructing your children that "hitting or fighting back" is inappropriate and could potentially make the situation worse.

5. Enrolling your child in a martial arts class is another method for building not only a child's self-confidence so that he/she is better prepared in the event of finding him/herself in frightening situations, but also providing your child to strengthen his/her mind, body and soul. By selecting an instructor that focuses on teaching children effective methods of removing themselves from difficult or dangerous situations without the use of physical contact, or at least a minimum, your child will be less likely to become a target.

Bullies are likely to always be around. And although you may "conquer" the desire for one bully to target you, there is always a good chance that there will be another one waiting in line. Determining exit strategies is paramount to the success your child will find in avoiding conflicts with bullies. These strategies can also be implemented when faced with difficult or dangerous situations. Reviewing these strategies with your child, again role playing is recommended.

Five Steps for Handling Bullies

1. Ignore the bullies attempts to "target & victimize" you. If you don't respond or react to his "jabs", he has no control over you as you've taken the thrill of bullying from   him.

2. Move away (toward a friendlier environment) from the area while continuing to ignore the bully. Moving somewhat quickly is a good idea without the appearance of running or fear because "bullies smell fear".

3. If the bully persists, utilizing the skills taught as a part of your "image makeover", turn around, look the bully square in the eyes and ask him to stop. Now, most bullies will push your buttons at this point or at least try too. For example, "what are you going to do if I don't?" Be prepared to either a) turn or walk away without a providing a response (because then he knows he's got you); or b) move onto step #4.

4. Again, if the bully continues, which he likely will, "strike a strong posture", make eye contact and use a firm voice once again only this time you'll TELL the bully to stop. This will probably catch him off guard. Some bullies are very stubborn and in fact may continue to try to push your buttons.

5. Without providing any further opportunity for confrontation, turn and walk away. Immediately tell an adult. At this point, your child should feel empowered as he just eliminated the power that the bully had over him/her.

If your child is still unable to take the steps that you've role-played and practiced or if they prove ineffective, it would be wise for you as a parent to step in and discuss the matter privately with the school's counselor, administrator and teacher.

Parents, NEVER ignore the non-verbal or verbal cues from your child that he/she is being tormented or is in some sort of trouble. Remember to ALWAYS be supportive, encouraging and most of all sympathetic to their situation. Provide plenty of hugs (if your child will permit them) and remind them how much you love them and want to help them learn to protect themselves. NEVER insult your child for being bullied as it may lead to your child feeling helpless and/or rejected by you. Bullying is serious business and can lead to serious consequences. Teaching and taking the necessary steps in advance, even if your child isn't being bullied, is always wise in preparing your child so that he/she can defend him/herself against becoming a potential target for bullies.

Since the first introduction of Susan Boyle on Britain's Got Talent, she has become a household name. Below is a heartfelt story of her struggles with bullies as a child.

*www.entertainmentwise.com/…/Susan-Boyle-I-Was-Beaten-And-**Bullied-As-A-Child***

CHAPTER THREE

WHAT BEGINS WITH THE LETTER "C"?

Fishing or rather "Catching" with Kids!

"One fish. Two fish. Red fish. Blue fish. Black fish. Blue fish. Old fish. New fish. This one has a little star. This one has a little car. Say! What a lot of fish there are." Dr. Seuss

Teaching a child to fish can be a fantastic experience for all participants - except perhaps the fish! Enjoying time together while learning the basics of fishing, although I prefer to call it "catching", can be one of the most memorable times an adult and child can experience together - or not.

I began fishing when I was extremely young. My grandfather took me regularly and I also fished with my family. We'd have fishing contests in which we'd earn points for 1) first catch of the day; 2) most fish caught; and 3) biggest fish. Being competitive and EXTREMELY patient, I usually won the contest as others in the competition would bore easily and I'd fish for hours. Not much has changed in that department. I'll still win virtually any fishing contest with my family, due in part because I'll "CATCH" for hours while they give up and swim, eat or whatever they can find to do in or around the boat. I have enjoyed fishing my entire life and no matter when or where I'm fishing, I'm reminded of the wonderful times had as a child.

Fishing is not for those with a short attention span unless you're in an area catching where they're practically jumping into the boat. We found this to be the case in an area down near Indian Rocks in Florida. On our last fishing trip, I'd literally throw out my line, give it a "jerk" and bring in a King Mackerel. It was truly an awesome fishing experience.

Now this isn't typical for most fishing trips. In fact, there have been days when we've barely caught a thing - notice I said barely. Luckily for me, I've got great friends and loved ones in wonderful places who always see to it that there is always a fish on the end of my line and that my fishing experiences are plentiful. Thanks Dad & Granddaddy!

When planning a fishing excursion, especially with children, you **MUST** know some basics. Grabbing a pole, some worms or crickets and heading out may prove unproductive if you aren't prepared with the proper gear, know-how, etc.... So, to help reduce the possibility of a dreaded adventure, you've got to do your homework! Let's begin with some basics.

Planning A Fishing Trip:

When planning a fishing trip, first things first.

1. ***Where are you going and how are you going to get there?*** Locating an acceptable spot for fishing is necessary. Never assume that just because there is a body of water that it's alright for you to fish in it. It might be privately owned or perhaps a body of water where fishing is prohibited. Just possibly, it might be located in an area where a fishing license is required - at least for the adult, or where a fee is paid allowing you to fish. Finally, the pond just over there may not be accessible by land and may require a boat. Do your homework ahead of time. Getting there - wherever there is needs some thought.

2. ***Are you fishing in salt water or fresh water?*** The type of fishing gear you'll need for your adventure will depend upon what you're fishing in and what you're fishing

for. Salt water gear is usually more heavy duty than freshwater fishing gear and designed not to rust. You'll still need to maintain your gear upon completion of your trip by rinsing it with fresh water to ensure that it doesn't deteriorate. Saltwater and sand can do ugly things to fishing equipment. You'll also need specific hooks, lures, line, and bait, etc....which is dependent upon what type(s) of fish you're fishing for. When fishing in saltwater, there are also limits to the number of specific fish as well as "seasons" for catching certain fish. Usually you can obtain a fishing guide in tackle and bait stores which will provide this information free of charge. They can also answer many of your questions regarding what's biting and what is being used to catch. Some salt and freshwater fish prefer live bait, while others will eat frozen bait. Then again, some fish you can only catch with artificial bait. Again, knowledge is a fish on the end of your hook. And remember, fishing licenses are required for saltwater fishing just like fishing in freshwater. Additionally, there are special licenses that are required for scallops, lobster, etc....and special tools that are required to assist in the humane removal of hooks and to release air trapped in the fish's bladder prior to releasing it back into the ocean. Freshwater fishing can be just as specific depending upon whether you're fishing in a river, pond, big lake or stream. There are many factors to consider including the water temperature, clarity, and current so you'll want to be really specific when preparing your tackle to go catching. Certain fish are more inclined to bite at different times of the day so you'll want to check the local fishing guide in order to make the most of your fishing excursion. Additionally, you'll need to check what "add-ons" you'll need on your freshwater fishing license, for instance a separate trout stamp, etc...And just like saltwater fishing, there are certain limits and sizes of fish that can be caught. Make certain that you are aware of the laws, limits and "cautions" when it comes to catching fish. Limits aren't just the law but are in place to protect individuals from consuming too many fish that contain higher levels of lead than others. Always do your homework.

3. *Planning your excursion.* Now that you know who, what, where, and why you're going fishing, you need to plan "when". Checking the weather forecast a few days in advance is always a wise idea. There is nothing worse than to prepare and build up one's expectations to go fishing only to have the weather modify or cancel your big plans. It is also a wise idea that should the weather forecast dish up something unexpected that you are prepared with an emergency weather radio, a method of

contacting the coast guard or other emergency services should an accident occur or should you need rescue services, and foul weather gear for both you and anyone else on board. Safety should always come first. Anyone who owns a boat knows that the unexpected can happen so being prepared is key!!! Make certain that if you are on a boat you have life vests, a floatation device geared for tossing in the event someone goes overboard  (attached to a rope that you maintain control over), plenty of water to ensure proper hydration, flares are always a good idea especially if you're in the ocean or large body of water, and miscellaneous tools and items for minor boat repairs should your boat stall or become disabled.

4. ***Notify others of your plans***. Be prepared!!! Always make certain that you let someone who is reliable know of your destination and plans. It is better to put everything in writing and leave it with someone that you can trust to be on the lookout for you and your return. If you modify your destination and/or plans, it is always best to let the individual know of this modification so that they are alert to your arrival and return.

5. ***Teaching your child the basics.*** Fishing can be fun for everyone IF they know the basics. This depends upon the age and physical fine motor dexterity of your child. You wouldn't expect a four year old to tie on a hook and bait it; however, a child that is seven years of age can certainly be taught basics. Tying a hook onto the line is one of those basics. You will want to ensure that the hook is tied on securely so the "big one" doesn't get away. You'll NEVER live that one down. You can also teach a child to put the bait on the hook which will inevitably be met with resistance. But, if you don't, you won't be fishing for the duration of the trip as you'll be responsible for replacing the bait every five seconds. Teaching your child about weight(s), floats, artificial and live bait are good to do and can be done early in age. Although depending on your child's age, teaching the child to remove the hook from the fish is something else you might want to do. Always have a net on board to prevent or eliminate losing a fish while he/she removes the hook - it might just make you a hero.

Fishing is a real adventure and can be one that continues throughout a lifetime if the proper measures are taken to ensure its success. When camping in Florida a few years ago we came upon a few boys who were attempting to fish from a bridge located over brackish water. Other than turtles and moccasins, which they caught, were black bream and plenty of them. After several hours of unsuccessful fishing they'd caught nothing - besides the moccasin which they'd snagged on their hook. We stopped and inquired what they were using to fish and they showed us the most messed up contraption we'd ever seen. They had various fishing lines tied to one another, hooks larger than the fish they were hoping to catch and floats that a grouper would have a hard time pulling beneath the water's surface (if you used them to catch grouper).

Apparently their parents didn't fish and had little interest in teaching them to do so. In an effort to experience it, they'd collected everything and anything that they could find and created their rigs to the best of their ability. Recognizing that they'd be lucky to snag anything desirable, we stripped their lines and prepared them with the proper fishing gear. Our sons also decided to fish alongside the boys and together caught 54 keepers. Because they'd never fished before, we inquired as to whether they'd ever eaten fish. Surprisingly, the amazing response was "No". In disbelief as the boys were FROM Florida, we offered to have a fish fry and cook up their catch as well as prepare side dishes and invited the kids and their families to join us.

Cleaning your Catch:

After a bountiful day of fishing, and unless you've chartered a fishing excursion, comes cleaning and cooking the fish. This is a messy job but somebody's got to do it. Luckily, my sons have learned to clean and fillet the fish so I no longer have the job (so sad!!) On the afternoon of the fishing adventure shared by all the kids, the boys eagerly cleaned and prepared the fish for the cookout. Learning the proper way to clean fish is something that everyone who is fishing for food should know how to do. You can obtain the information in books or online or if you're lucky you can observe someone who knows how to do it and learn from the experience.

If you've fished all day and caught ANYTHING you'll want to let the child experience eating it. If the child is young, you may want to avoid letting him or her see you kill and fillet the fish. For some children it is a traumatic experience. Usually by the time the child is eight years of age, they are able to understand the concept of killing ONLY what we intend to eat.

Eating your Catch:

As anyone who's eaten fish before knows, there are hundreds of bones inside. Whether filleted or not, if you don't know how to fillet and you've chosen to fry the entire fish, please instruct your child about chewing small portions at a time and really being careful about swallowing the bones. It is quite frightening and painful when one gets by and becomes lodged in your throat.

Note: Should a bone be swallowed and it feels lodged within the throat, and if you cannot visually see it than it is probably too low within the throat to remove. So, eating a wad of bread with peanut butter will usually result in its passing. The sensation of the bone being stuck may continue as it has irritated the esophagus.

Good Side Dishes to Accompany your Catch:

Loving to eat is something that I know I'm not alone in and the sky's the limit when it comes to foods that can "spice up" a good fish dinner. Whether it is freshwater or saltwater fish, a good southern favorite is cheese grits. Yep, you heard me correct. Good ole slow cooked grits with salt & cheese added to them (oh yes, and use milk instead of water!!!). You can even add a little red or cayenne pepper to taste - if kids are eating them - you may want to cook a separate batch. In Florida, we like to prepare (in the summer) some fresh sliced tomatoes although some folks like to eat fried green tomatoes instead. You've got to have sweet pickles too.

There are many other delectable foods to go along with fish too. Some people enjoy some form of chowder, etouffee, seasoned rice & beans, or simply rice. Others like hushpuppies, French fries, steamed or grilled vegetables, and even jambalaya. I for one like a good potato salad with fish while my husband loves coleslaw. There are times when fish just aren't enough and you need to have shrimp, crabs or crab cakes or crab stuffing, etc...Remember, there are literally dozens of delicious side dishes to accompany a good fish fry (or broiled, baked, blackened piece of fish).

Note: Before eating or serving fish, shellfish, etc....to individuals, know whether they have food allergies.

Remember, fishing is a wonderful thing to teach a child or anyone to do. It is an opportunity to spend quality time with those that you love and I promise, if you've done your homework and made the trip a pleasant one (even if you didn't catch anything) your child will remember it with fondness one day. It's more about the time spent together than about what ends up on the end of your hook (although, catching does taste sweeter than going home with an empty cooler.)

Oh yes, one more tip!!! You MUST ALWAYS (unless it violates the law) Kiss & Keep your first catch - no matter what. It's good luck and will ensure a day plentiful of fish, if not for you, someone in the boat!

And remember -If you give a person a fish, they'll eat for a day. But if you train a person to fish, they'll fish for a lifetime.
-Author Unknown

Happy Fishing!!!

For assistance in planning your fishing trip, visit your local Bass Pro Shop, Outdoor World or other specialty fishing store. They will have the gear, knowledge and "tips" to make your fishing adventure a huge success.

REMEMBER TO TAKE YOUR CAMERA - IF THEY CATCH THE BIG ONE AND YOU BELIEVE IN CATCH & RELEASE, YOU CAN ALWAYS KEEP A PHOTO OF THE MOMENT!!!

You can also document the actual size of the fish to go along with the gigantic fishing stories that will follow.

"When you are on the river, ocean or in the woods, you are the closest to the truth you'll ever get." Jack Leonard

Effective Classroom Management

With today's economy which frequently includes budget cuts, additional job responsibilities and furloughs the last thing a teacher needs are the complications resulting from ineffective classroom management.

Classroom management does not begin the minute the children walk through the door but actually starts with the overall plan that should be designed for not only the arrangement of furnishings, books and materials but with the routine, flow and structure that you intend to utilize once students are present.

In order to effectively manage a classroom, a teacher should have a clear understanding of the how's, what's, where's and when's as they apply to multiple factors including storage of your student's belongings such as lunches & book bags, where the students will submit their class & homework assignments, and the best location for trash cans and pencil sharpeners as well as various work stations and the "teacher's" desk.

Let's begin with organizing the flow to effectively accommodate the movement of your students without disturbing countless others. In other words, let's minimize opportunities for misbehavior and off-task behavior(s).

The first consideration after that of establishing your teaching philosophy and behavioral strategies should be developing a floor plan that will work comfortably to allow for your instructional style and/or plans to flow smoothly. What this means is that you will need to arrange furniture in a manner that will allow you to do everything without the need to re-arrange and/or move furniture which may result in injury to you and/or others.

For instance, depending upon the furnishings provided, you'll need to decide how you will arrange the student's work-spaces for independent and group work, if you intend to utilize cooperative work groups and/or learning stations. Seating arrangements can be the single most important criteria for managing a classroom full of children and can be a real challenge. For example, some schools provide individual desks while others provide oversized tables meant for accommodating multiple students. Depending upon your teaching style and methodology, this can pose a real challenge.

After determining the best layout for your student's desks, determining a convenient location for work stations or centers, classroom supplies, the pencil sharpener, trash cans, and various other items to be utilized throughout the course of daily instruction. Many factors will dictate where some of the basics will need to be located such as the space available within your room. Convenience is important but so is maintaining control of your children as it relates to their movement(s) in and around the classroom.

A critical point to understand *is proximity to other students being a tremendous factor in classroom management.* I found that by placing (1) trash can near my desk I was able to eliminate a great deal of misbehavior. I placed the remaining trash can beneath the pencil sharpener to contain messes waiting to happen. I also stored classroom materials and supplies beside my desk to prevent students from gathering and becoming disruptive to others working independently. As basic as this may sound, you'd be surprised at how many teachers have trouble with these two very basic areas within classroom management.

After establishing the best locations for resources that will be used by many, determining centralized location(s) for the storage of individual student's items is critical. While at the middle and high school level lockers are usually provided and serve this purpose, in elementary school you're typically left with desks in which to store small items or wall hooks and/or cubbies for storing personal items. As much as we'd like to believe that children's items will be safe & sound wherever their things are stored, the reality is that something will disappear from time to time with absolutely no explanation or evidence as to its whereabouts and is a serious problem in many schools. In an effort to reduce the possibility of this occurrence, choosing a visible location that will prevent someone's ability to remove other person's things unnoticed will serve you well. It is best to make sure the area is visible from most, if not all, angles and is not located near the doorway.

Next, you'll want to establish learning centers and/or stations such as your reading corner or area, listening stations, manipulatives area, etc... Again, keep in mind the need to strategically place these areas so that you can visibly see all activities underway as well as allowing for the best usage of space, electrical outlets as needed, lighting, non-carpeted or carpeted space, and the number of children that will utilize the spaces at any given time.

In my classroom, I built a loft which provided space both upstairs and down (similar to the concept of a bunkbed) for various activities. Upstairs was used as a reading loft while the lower level served as a listening station and sometimes as a puppetry stage or center. My classroom library was conveniently located beside the loft for children to access books. Across the room I established my manipulatives and blocks area to keep the noisier activities from disturbing the more quite spaces. All manipulatives were stored in this space including games, cards, blocks, letter tiles, stacking cubes, etc... I think you are probably getting the idea so I will move forward.

A teacher is a trained professional who is probably one of the most competent multi-taskers on the planet alongside mothers. Recognizing the importance of a proper, safe and organized classroom floorplan is paramount to the management of students and various ongoing activities at any given time. By carefully planning, in advance, how your reading center in relation to the block area, and/or student's storage space as it relates to entry and exit points, plus all of the other specific details as they relate to your individual teaching style, you can potentially avoid many pitfalls in which many teachers find themselves.

The rest is up to you.

I've taken the liberty of attaching an illustration of a classroom floorplan which is demonstrative of one providing proper flow and allowing for a variety of learning opportunities within a limited amount of space. Every teacher will have different needs; however, sometimes seeing an effective layout design will provide you the "something" that you couldn't quite put your finger upon when designing your classroom. I hope it will prove helpful to you or one of your fellow teachers.

Curing Sinus Infections the Natural Way

Flu season is when so many children (and adults) are diagnosed with colds, the flu, strep throat, viral infections AND sinus infections also known as Sinusitis. The typical scenario is that the child complains of a symptom, mom/dad treats it with over-the-counter medications which, on occasion, have positive results. Sometimes too much time passes requiring the child (or adult) visit a physician where he/she is prescribed medication(s) which will ultimately cure the illness but usually for a small fortune and typically after many prescriptions have been filled.

What if you could prevent the onset of illnesses by making positive changes in your lifestyle and diet? It is possible and is absolutely the best option available for families in the prevention of illnesses running rampant in their homes and/or the lives of our families.

If you are scratching your head and asking yourself, "How can a few changes in my lifestyle and diet make a difference in whether I become ill or not?" the answer is short and simple: Eating healthy leads to a healthy body and stronger immune system. A strong immune system allows your body to fight off and destroy germs before they are able to attack your body and make themselves at home. I've prepared *Ten Tips on What You Can Do to Avoid a Cold & Flu* which can be found in **Children Topics from A to Z**, Volume 2.

Now, in the event that you contract a sinus infection, aka sinusitis, there are other options available to you. Aside from the healthy eating habits and lifestyle referenced above, there are many natural remedies that can be used to treat sinusitis and best of all; they don't require a trip to the doctor or a prescription. Each of the remedies have been tried, tested and true and will often be able to eliminate the ailments without the need for antibiotics which are known to *destroy* "good bugs" along with the "bad bugs". Additionally, they destroy your intestinal tract flora **severely impairing digestion and assimilation of nutrients** at a time when your body needs them most.

First, let's review what **Sinusitis** actually is. It is a condition often considered an infection or inflammation of the para-nasal sinuses. It may or may not be the result of infection from bacterial, fungal, viral, allergic or autoimmune issues. It is considered to be highly contagious and can be passed from one individual to another through direct contact with an infected surface or transmitted through the air. The most common symptoms of sinusitis are constant or excessive sneezing, low grade fever, runny nose, headache, blockage of one or both nostrils, and pressure around the eyes, head, and face. Lack of appetite and difficulty in breathing are other symptoms of sinusitis.

Now that we know what it is (or is not) let's review several home remedies that you can use that are safe, non-toxic, effective and provide the same results as antibiotics WITHOUT affecting the "internal" workings of our intestinal system.

Natural Remedies for Curing Sinus Infections (Sinusitis):

- **Organic Apple Cider Vinegar:** This is the best home remedy around - and it has been around for many years. Not to disclose my age, but let's just say I learned about it when I was a child and that was 30+ years ago. How does it work? We really don't know but the concept behind the remedy is to actually take it immediately upon feeling the sniffles, stuffiness, allergies, colds, flu and pain and pressure coming on so that you catch it before it becomes a full blown infection. Taken as a daily tonic or at the first sign of an allergy or cold, this remedy can put the brakes on the histamine response or allergic reaction. There are a few ways to take it: 1) Pour 1/8 to 1/4 cup in 16 ounces of water and sip it throughout the day (you can also drink it warm like tea). 2) You can take 2 Tablespoons mixed with water - swallowing it very quickly. If you already have a sinus infection, drink the mixture for a couple of days along with plenty of water and it should clear it up. Apple Cider Vinegar thins mucus almost immediately. The thinning of mucus is the key to eliminating your sinus infection. Once the mucus is thinned, you can follow the treatment plan using the remedies below.

- **Grapefruit Seed Extract:** Along with the remedy above, a few days of grapefruit seed extract will make your infection disappear. Grapefruit seed extract is very potent. It is recommended that you use the drop formulation but be aware that they taste horrible!!! Never take them on an empty stomach, especially first thing in the morning. About 2 - 5 tiny drops will do the trick.

- **Raw vegetable juice** is beneficial in treating sinusitis. Combine 300 ml of carrot juice, 100 ml of cucumber juice, 100 ml of beet juice and 200 ml of spinach juice and drink it daily.

- Roast 100 grams of **cumin seeds** and mix them with 200 grams of pure ghee. What is GHEE? Ghee is clarified butter -- the butter oil, without the lactose and other milk solids. Consume daily. ***It is one of the most effective ways to cure sinusitis.***

- **Steam** is effective in curing sinusitis. It opens the nasal passage by draining the sinuses and making mucous flow easy.

- **Prepare ginger or cinnamon tea** and drink it when it is slightly on the hotter side. It is helpful in curing sinusitis.

- **Saline solutions** are also wonderful in treating and thinning mucus within the passages. This can be made by adding a pinch of sea salt to lukewarm water and misting within your nose. Drops will work as well.

- **Inhaling steam with either Apple Cider Vinegar or Cayenne Pepper** mixed in will also help to loosen and thin the mucus. Blowing your nose to rid your sinus passages of the mucus will help to eliminate it from your system.

- **Green Tea with 1T crushed or powdered Ginger, 1T Lime Juice, and 1t Honey** is also known to help with the inflammation in and around the ears reducing pressure and promoting the draining of fluids which ultimately become the problem in the sinus cavity. This is a practice that I encourage parents to use with children whom the Ear, Nose and Throat doctor has recommended surgery to help reduce or eliminate this repetitive illness through the removal of the glands.

- Finally, if you still feel that you have an excessive amount of mucus **try modifying your diet.** For instance, eliminate all mucus-forming/thickening foods and/or drinks for a couple of days. These foods include milk, citrus, spicy foods, wheat, cheese, etc....as they are the typical culprits.

Natural remedies are readily available for most illnesses if you're willing to do a little homework to find them. They are natural, effective and usually resolve the illness quicker than pharmaceutical methods and without the side-effects so commonly experienced through the use of pharmaceutical drugs. Do not eliminate visiting a medical professional simply because there are other options available. Sometimes medical professionals are simply not necessary.

If your illness is severe and/or not responding to the at-home treatments above, you might need to seek professional medical assistance for another opinion or treatment option.

CHAPTER FOUR

WHAT BEGINS WITH THE LETTER "D"?

Teenage Depression - Symptoms and Solutions

As difficult as it is to imagine, teenage depression is serious business. From the adult's perspective, the teenage years are some of the greatest times in life. From a teenagers view, it can be quite the opposite.

Depression encompasses every aspect of a teen's life - and often his or her family's too. It isn't just mood swings but also involves frequent bouts of sadness, discouragement, a lack or loss of self-worth and usually is associated with a loss of interest in usual activities once enjoyed by the teen. Without treatment, teen depression will often result in serious problems at school and home; drug and alcohol abuse by many teens; self-destructive attitudes and behaviors; and sometimes, homicidal violence or suicide.

What Causes Depression?

There are many factors that contribute to teenage depression. Some are psychological in nature while others physiological. For instance, it might simply be a particular situation or disturbing event that has the teen up-in-arms and out-of-sorts. Maybe your teen just broke up with a boyfriend or girlfriend; suffered a recent loss of a family member, friend or pet; or maybe he or she is struggling academically at school.

It may be linked to the maturation process and the stresses that go hand-in-hand with normal development. Often, it can be attributed to sex hormones wreaking havoc on your teen's system resulting in physical, emotional and social issues or stresses or even something as simple as a teen's need for independence and the conflicts that often result with parents. Other risk factors that have been linked to teen depression:

- Physical and/or sexual abuse
- Severe and/or chronic illness

- Inherited - family history of depression
- Inept social skills
- Loss of a parent (death or divorce)
- Extremely stressful events or pressures in life
- Inconsistent parenting and/or caregiving

Depression is ugly anyway you look at it and can deeply alter a teenager's personality. This is not to say that your teen will not occasionally fall victim to a bad mood or acting out behaviors - that's human nature. Should a teen experience more "downs" than "ups", you might want to know what you're looking for in terms of frequent and common symptoms associated with teenage depression.

Symptoms of Teenage Depression:

There are many symptoms of teen depression and some can be misconstrued and/or misread. So, the key is recognizing on average how often your child experiences the symptoms that have you concerned. But first, recognizing normal signs of moodiness as experienced by teens who are going through puberty, trying to determine "who" they are and "where" they fit in need to be eliminated from the mix.

Normal transition from child to teenager to adult will often be trying for both teens and their parents, especially when they attempt to distinguish and/or assert their independence. Recognizing "normal" teenage behavior and behaviors that aren't necessarily a part of the maturation process can be tricky. Let's identify the most common signs and symptoms of depression as experienced by teenagers.

Common Signs & Symptoms of Teenage Depression:

- Deep seated feeling of worthlessness, sadness or hopelessness
- Anger, hostility or irritability
- Difficulty concentrating
- Frequent tearfulness or crying
- Decreased energy
- Inability to sleep (insomnia) & Chronic fatigue
- Loss of interest & general lack of motivation and enthusiasm
- Avoidance of family and friends

- Increased restlessness and agitation (bad temper)
- Changes in appetite (more often a loss than an increase)
- Irresponsible behavior pattern (missed curfews, unusual defiance)
- Weight change - either loss or gain (unintentional)
- Academic difficulties & performance
- Substance abuse (drugs, alcohol or even smoking cigarettes)
- Illegal activities - shoplifting; arson; vandalism
- Thoughts about suicide or obsessive fears or worries about dying
- Suicidal tendencies or actual suicide attempt

Each of these symptoms and/or signs can be indicative of teenage depression AND typical teenage behavior. If the symptoms are severe, meaning that they are substantially different for your teen, and if they are consistently present for a period of at least two to four weeks, and are significant in terms of your child's personality, mood and/or behavior, you may want to consider professional counseling and/or medical advice.

Treating Teenage Depression:

Left untreated, teenage depression can have long-lasting negative, dangerous and even fatal results. If you feel that your teen is struggling with teenage depression, seek assistance from a medical professional as often it is difficult to diagnose this illness in teens. A medical professional will complete a physical examination, order blood work to rule out medical causes for the symptoms. Additionally, the doctor will perform routine tests to determine if there are any signs of substance abuse such as heavy drinking, the use of marijuana or other drugs in his/her system.

After the medical examination is complete (should it not provide any results linking to depression) you'll want to consider a psychiatric evaluation. This will document your teen's history in terms of sadness, irritability, loss of interest and enjoyment of life's normal activities. During this evaluation, the doctor will also attempt to discover any coexisting disorders such as anxiety, mania or schizophrenia. This in-depth evaluation will be completed in order to determine if there is a risk of suicide or homicidal tendencies. In other words, this will determine whether or not the teenager is a threat to himself or others. The medical professionals may seek information from family members, teachers, or other school personnel in order to make a complete assessment of the child.

Upon completion of the various assessments, a treatment plan will be recommended. This will depend upon the diagnosis, the severity and nature of the symptoms. It may include supportive care from a medical provider, perhaps psychotherapy, and perhaps antidepressant medications often referred to as selective serotonin reuptake inhibitors (SSRI). Please note that SSRI's address the possible increase and/or risk of suicidal thoughts and actions by children and adolescents. If your teen is prescribed therapy, it is sometimes recommended that families participate especially in the event that family conflict is a contributing factor to the teen's depression.

Effective Strategies for Talking to a Depressed Teen:

Unfortunately, teenagers who are suffering from depression aren't always "amenable" to conversations with others - especially as it pertains to their depression and symptoms. So, how do you attempt to "reach out" when your teen is "pulling away"? The first thing that you'll want to do is let your child know how much you love him/her. Then, without being judgmental, share your concerns including specific signs of depression that you've observed your child demonstrating. Encourage your child to share with you what he/she is feeling or what is affecting him/her in such a dramatic manner.

Here are (4) effective strategies for talking to your depressed teenager:

1. **Offer Support** - Without pressing or imposing, make certain that your teenager realizes that you're there for him/her - no matter what! Teenagers don't like when parents ask too many questions and/or pry, so let him/her know that you're there and available whenever they're ready to talk.
2. **Gentle Persistence** - Teenagers are known for "shutting the door" on communication - it's their age so when this happens, and it more than likely will - "don't give up." The topic of depression is a tough one to swallow, especially for teenagers. Consider your teen's comfort level when it comes to discussing "touchy" topics and allow them to share when ready.
3. **Listen, Listen, Listen** - When your teenager is ready to "open up" and share with you whatever it is that is bothering him/her, it is your responsibility to "LISTEN". You may feel inclined to offer advice or even judge - DON'T DO IT! You must resist the urge if you truly want your teenager to talk freely with you

about their issue(s). Communication is the key - without it, you'll more than likely never understand what has your child so upset.

4. **Validation** - Everyone, young and old, needs acknowledgment. It will take a lot of courage on the part of your teenager to open up and share, whether you feel that their "issues" are valid or irrational. It isn't up to you to judge - it is up to you to validate the feelings being shared and express a genuine concern. Acknowledge the pain and sadness that your child is feeling and under NO circumstance should you take on the role of counselor and attempt to talk your teen out of his/her depression. They need to feel that you honestly care about what they're sharing with you.

Some teens may not "come clean" about what is going on in their lives. Remember, just because your teen denies anything is wrong doesn't necessarily mean "nothing" is wrong. You know your child better than anyone and if you suspect something isn't quite right, allow your instincts to take the lead. Denial is a very strong emotion - especially when it comes to teenage depression (like that of drug use, alcoholism, hoarding, etc.…).

Teenagers suffering from depression won't necessarily understand what is happening to them. So, if you notice that your teen is behaving in a manner that isn't customary for him/her, you may need to take a closer look. Unfortunately, for some teens, their signs and symptoms go unnoticed and the end result isn't good. In fact, the danger of suicide in some teens is substantial. Knowing what warning signs to listen and look for in a depressed teenager is critical for all parents. Below is a list to be aware of:

<u>Warning Signs of Suicide:</u>

- Jokes or frequent conversations/statements about committing suicide;
- Comments or statements such as, "I wish I could just disappear", or "There's no way out!" and "I'd be better off dead!"
- Romanticizing death and dying, i.e. "If I were dead, maybe I'd be missed."
- Writing poetry, lyrics or stories about death, dying and suicide.
- Frequent accidents resulting in unexplained injury; uncommon reckless behavior.
- Giving away items of significance to others;
- Unexplained "goodbyes" to family, friends and loved ones;
- Sudden desire to obtain weapons, pills or other means used for killing oneself.

Warning signs are just that - a warning that your child is "thinking" about killing him/herself. Don't ignore the signs!!! If you hear or observe your child referencing death, suicide or any of the other "warning signs" above, take it seriously and as a cry for help. These cries for help are significant! You'll want to act immediately but without alarming, and/or startling your teen. This could lead to a higher level of frustration or stress within your child.

Your child, whether depressed or not, should always receive your support - no matter what he/she is going through. If your child is suffering from depression, you'll want to ensure that he/she has more support now than ever before. It will be tiring and often frustrating, but it will definitely be worth the end result(s).

What You Can Do to Help Your Teenager Through His or Her Treatment:

- **Be Understanding.** Your teenager is suffering. You'll need to exercise great patience and a higher than usual level of understanding. Remember, he/she isn't being difficult intentionally.
- **Encourage Physical Activity.** Staying active is an excellent method of relieving symptoms of depression. Make certain that it is a part of your teen's daily life.
- **Social Activity.** Although your teen may feel like being isolated, isolation only makes the symptoms of depression worse. You'll want to encourage that he/she remain socially engaged with others.
- **Remain Actively Involved in Treatment**. Your child needs to recognize that you're going to be with him/her every step of the way - this is especially important if your child is involved in any form of treatment/therapy. You'll want to be aware of the suggestions and strategies that the therapist and/or Doctor is implementing so that you can ensure that your teen is following through with them.
- **Learn everything you can about Depression**. You'll want to make certain that you are educated as much as possible about teenage depression, therapy, medication, side-effects, and anything else that are available to you. It is also wise to help your child learn as much too. With knowledge comes a great deal of power. The power to heal comes through knowledge.

Teenage depression can be a scary thing - especially for the child who suffers from it. It will be difficult for the entire family and anyone involved. Living with depression will require a great deal of patience, empathy and compassion on everyone's part. Make certain that the entire family understands that the treatment process will be long and have both its ups and downs. It is always best to have a "game plan" in place so that every member of the family understands how they can contribute in a positive manner. Remember, your teenager is the same child whose hand you held in the beginning - you'll need to hold it again until your child feels that he/she can walk again. Don't let go until he/she is ready!

Saying "NO" to Drugs

Every time I hear the word "drugs" I cringe as usually the word is followed by child, adolescent or teenager and often it is something devastating. No matter the lengths to which adults go to teach their children about the dangers of drugs and alcohol, inevitably children are drawn to the harmful substances, sometimes illegal, that are prevalent on the streets, in our homes and other locations. Does this mean that we should simply "give up" and develop the attitude that they're going to try them anyway? Of course not and in fact it should inspire us to try that much harder to inspire them to live above the influence.

A Different Drug Problem:

Once upon a time, there was a different kind of drug problem. This problem appeals to me and somewhat reminded me of my youth. I wanted to share the story entitled "Different Drug Problem" which was submitted by a concerned citizen to a newspaper in Avoyelles Parish. Please read on:

"The other day, someone at a store in our town read that a Methamphetamine lab had been found in an old farmhouse in the adjoining county and he asked me a rhetorical question, "Why didn't we have a drug problem when you and I were growing up?"

"I replied I had a drug problem when I was young: I was drug to church on Sunday morning. I was drug to church for weddings and funerals. I was drug to family reunions and community socials no matter the weather."

"I was drug by my ears when I was disrespectful to adults. I was also drug to the woodshed when I

disobeyed my parents, told a lie, brought home a bad report card, did not speak with respect, spoke ill of the teacher or the preacher, or if I didn't put forth my best effort in everything that was asked of me."

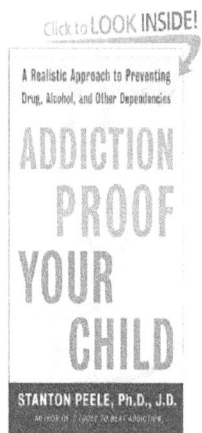

"I was drug to the kitchen sink to have my mouth washed out with soap if I uttered a profanity. I was drug out to pull weeds in mom's garden and flower beds and cockleburs out of dad's fields. I was drug to the homes of family, friends and neighbors to help out some poor soul who had no one to mow the yard, repair the clothesline, or chop some firewood, and, if my mother had ever known that I took a single dime as a tip for this kindness, she would have drug me back to the woodshed.

"Those drugs are still in my veins and they affect my behavior in everything I do, say or think. They are stronger than cocaine, crack, or heroin; and, if today's children had this kind of drug problem, America would be a better place. God bless the parents who drugged us."

Drugs are a real problem with youth and adults. Often it isn't "street drugs" that people are turning to but chemicals within our homes that provide kids with a "buzz". Here are some interesting facts and details about "drugs" today.

Why Children (and some adults) Use Drugs:

Believe it or not, it isn't always the influence of peers, adults or drug dealers that encourage or influence children to use drugs. A group of children who used drugs were questioned about the reason behind their desire to use them. Their responses might surprise and even alarm you. They were:

- I'm bored - Drugs help me relieve boredom
- To make me feel good
- To help me forget my troubles and allow me to relax and/or sleep
- They help me have fun be reducing my inhibitions
- Because I wanted to see what it was like to be "high", "excited", etc...
- I'm able to do things when I'm stoned that I wouldn't otherwise do.
- It makes the pain go away.
- I wanted to feel like a grown-up.
- To exercise my independence.

- It makes me look cool.
- If I do drugs, I am a part of a group.

Recognizing some of the reasons "why" children elect to experiment with drugs may assist parents in providing healthy alternatives to self-medicating and drug use by their children. As parents, familiarizing yourself with the list of explanations above and then listening to and watching your own children will be a great help in the prevention of your child's use of drugs.

Healthy Alternatives to Drugs:

Parents are the best judge of character when it comes to their children. Now this is not to say that some parents will recognize or even acknowledge that their child may have a problem as some parents are living in denial or refuse to see the writing on the wall. That is not an insult to those parents but more of an observation. It's easier not to see what others may see. It's how people protect themselves from things that are difficult to hear, acknowledge and sometimes deal with. The real concern here is, easier for whom? Definitely NOT the child!!!

Being "in tune with" the trends that children are drawn to is something that every parent should be up-to-date and aware of. Having a clear understanding of the mischief in which young children will engage to alleviate boredom, to make them "feel" popular or whatever the case may be is mandatory, especially if your child tends to be a follower, suffer from low self-esteem, lacks close personal friendships with peers, etc...

In many cases, children will provide telltale signs of their unhappiness or their impending path into trouble. If your child often complains about being bored, which most of them do, perhaps encouraging him/her to become involved in sports, clubs, community service projects and/or organizations, church or youth group activities, or engaged in some form of lessons i.e. dance, music, art, etc....would be beneficial. Keeping children active, engaged and interested in various extra-curricular events will not only provide your child the opportunity to build interpersonal relationships and skills, but will also allow them to build or strengthen their confidence.

Self-confidence typically leads down a different path than a lack thereof. Just because your child repeats that he/she is bored doesn't automatically indicate that he/she will experiment with drugs, but by providing alternatives before boredom sets in will certain reduce the possibility. Additionally, by involving your child in worthwhile activities, he/she will establish relationships with other adults, peers and their parents which will allow each to influence the child in more positive ways. "Rise above the influence" couldn't be more evident than through improved relationships with parents, siblings and peers.

Drug Use by Children Is More Common Than Many Realize:

Many parents live sheltered lives when it comes to drugs and their child's use and/or knowledge of them. The phrase, "My child doesn't even know what drugs are...she's only in the second grade!" Or, "We live in a close-knit neighborhood/community where drugs aren't a factor because they aren't available." Guess what - these parents couldn't be more at a loss in what their children actually know and consider or USE as drugs.

In fact, when drugs were discussed within classrooms through various anti-drug programs such as, "D.A.R.E.", children as young as second and third grade had an overwhelming knowledge about inhalants and other popular street drugs such as marijuana, cocaine, and crystal meth as well as others. And these children were typical 7 and 8 year olds. More shocking is the fact that the students sharing the information are typically from upper class suburban homes. Statistically speaking, 34% of children ages 12 to 17-years of age who've used inhalants came from families earning anywhere from $40,000 to $80,000 per year with an additional one-third from families earning over $80,000 annually. From these statistics, seventy percent were Caucasian with an equal distribution between boys and girls.

Street drugs are not the only form of "drug" or "high" that children get their kicks from. In fact, they are turning to mom and dad's medicine cabinet and everyday household chemicals that are more easily accessible and which are perfect for "popping" and "sniffing". Yes, children have found a fascination in "sniffing" chemicals with the sole intent of getting a rush. In fact, the National Institute on Drug Abuse has noted that, "Inhaling chemicals can cause a quick, powerful high similar to the effects of drinking alcohol.

The symptoms are short-lived, so abusers often use the chemicals repeatedly to maintain their high." Children are targeting items that we wouldn't even dream of and they are making their way into the lives of children as young as 8 and 9 years of age. How they learn about some of these things is beyond my wildest imagination but they've figured it out and perhaps television programming or a peer who's been exposed to it by an older sibling is the culprit. There seems to be an overwhelming amount of information being shared amongst our children.

Some of the most popular Inhalants Children are Targeting:

- White-Out (the popular office supply) - children paint their fingernails with this common product and sniff their fingernails to obtain a high.
- Fabric protectors
- Acetone products like nail polish and polish removers.
- Nitrous oxide which is popular in whippets (Whipped Cream)
- Vegetable cooking sprays - who knew?
- Halon fire extinguishers
- Felt-tip Markers
- Glues and adhesives
- Butane
- Gasoline
- Air fresheners
- Spray Paint
- Lacquers
- Paint Thinners
- Hair Sprays (something most women have in their bathroom)

Discovering drug use, especially of the inhalant variety, are often difficult to determine if you aren't aware of the symptoms. Please familiarize yourself with the telltale signs associated with inhalant abuse. Share the information with your child's teachers, local school, other parents and even your children as you never know when your child may be in the presence of another child in danger.

Symptoms of Inhalant Abuse include:

- Chronic red or runny nose
- Unexplained sores or rash around the mouth or nose
- Nausea and headaches
- Chronic cough
- Sudden Memory loss and/or lack of concentration

- Chemical smell on the breath, clothes or in the bedroom or other commonly visited locations throughout the home.
- Paint stains on the clothing or skin.
- Soft drink cans, rags or sandwich bags with a chemical odor

Other symptoms include:

- Abrupt changes in academic performance and attendance
- Changes in personal hygiene habits
- Extreme mood swings
- Red, irritated eyes
- Sudden weight loss
- Loss of interest in friends, sports and even hobbies

Other Drug Trends to Be Aware of:

As children get older, we tend to allow more freedoms than we would when they were younger. This is especially true of high school students. Parents BEWARE!!! There is another equally, if not more dangerous drug trend on the horizon. It is referred to in our community as "Pharm" NOT "Farm" parties. Simply put: Children raid their parent's medicine cabinets and collect as many varieties of medication that they can obtain. They're smart enough NOT to take all of the pills within the bottle so as not to be discovered, but take enough that they end up with a substantial variety of highly potent, often deadly medications. Children then get together and collectively add the pills into a "serving bowl" then begin eating them as if they're eating M & M's. They literally consume handfuls of random medications which have proven fatal as lethal combinations take effect.

Most parents will agree that when under the influence many unpleasant and undesirable things can occur. This couldn't be truer than when a bunch of teenagers are experimenting with both drugs and alcohol. As if the consumption of drugs and alcohol isn't enough, the behaviors in which these teens engage would make your head spin 360 degrees. In fact, sometimes "Pharm" parties wind up becoming another trend among teens referred to as "Rainbow" parties. These parties are associated with a group of teenage girls wearing different shades of lipstick and then performing oral sex on one or more partners - the end result being a "rainbow" of color residues upon the recipient's private parts.

Finally, the age old favorite among teenagers, marijuana is being used in conjunction with powerful and more potent drugs lacing it. Again, the results are toxic and can be fatal as many children aren't aware of the dangerous levels of medications that they are combining for a "good" time.

Talk to Your Children about Drugs - It's NEVER too early.....

It's never too early to start talking to your children about drug use and the life-altering hazards associated with "experimental" drug use. The long-term effects of drug use, especially repeated use, can be devastating and children should be made aware of the dangers. They need to understand that accidents happen and that even improper use of and a single-episode can be fatal.

Children need to understand that "huffing" or "sniffing" inhalants, although in their minds a "harmless" experiment, have been linked to a significant increase leading to their future use of cocaine and heroin. Additionally, they need to be aware of the increased incidence of seizures, asphyxiation, comas, heart failure and death. The photo to the left, if clicked upon, will highlight many of the potential life-threatening and even fatal results of this activity.

Sharing the potential hazards associated with consuming prescription medicines (not prescribed for them) is something that every parent should address with their children. Children may see that the medications make you "better" or help your health improve NOT realizing that by consuming medications intended for treatment of a specific medical condition in one individual can actually result in complications, illness or death in another.

Keep your eyes and ears open and communicate with other parents on a regular basis. You'll be surprised to learn the things that transpire when groups of unsupervised children get together and even when "chaperones" are present. In fact, some of the most alarming events that have been shared with me were when adults were present but not necessarily - "present".

Know How to Say No to Drugs and Alcohol
A Kid's Guide

Please don't wait until it's too late. Speak to your children about

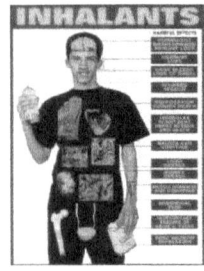 drug use. If you aren't sure how to approach your child about this topic, visit. The organization is operated by the National Inhalant Prevention Coalition and can provide helpful information. There are also kid friendly websites which provide information that your child can read should he/she prefer to read the information in lieu of a "lecture" from mom or dad (although it isn't a lecture in reality).

Perhaps getting back to basics such as "sitting down" at the table to eat meals with our families; spending weekends together at home enjoying the company and conversation with one another; and perhaps monitoring the exposure to television, internet, and other wireless forms of communication would help in our fight against drugs. It's a start and the health and well-being of our children depend upon us to make the changes to benefit all of us.

CHAPTER FIVE

WHAT BEGINS WITH THE LETTER "E"?

Making Excuses for Your Child's Actions and Behavior....

Setting the Stage:

Recently I had the misfortune of being on the receiving end of a child having a complete melt-down. The child, who has a history of violent and uncontrolled outbursts of anger and disruptive behavior, attempted to hurt a classmate while the child, along with his classmates were lining up on the sidewalk to return to the classroom. Unfortunately for the misbehaving child, his efforts to run over the classmate were foiled when he lost his balance while running behind and pushing a Tonka trunk toward the classmate standing in line with a speed far more than his coordination could handle. Instead of inflicting pain to the child he had targeted, he instead lost his balance, fell and skinned both his forehead and cheek on the stucco finish of the school's building. Immediately he began crying and screaming as if he'd been the victim.

Once we'd returned to the classroom from the playground I attempted to comfort the child who was obviously shaken. Each of my attempts to wipe away his tears, clean the scratches and/or calm him were met with anger as he knocked the tissues from my hands or threw whatever object he could obtain across the room. I attempted many times to comfort him, as regardless of the actions leading to his injury he needed not just emotional but medical attention. But he didn't want any part of it. Instead he, being not only the largest child in the class but also the strongest, picked up a chair and tossed it into the center of the group of children sitting on the carpet preparing themselves for center(s). Luckily his intended target(s) were missed and as I knelt down between he and the other children to prevent any further attempts to hurt someone, I received a blow to the cheek by the out-of-control child. Shaken, but still in control, I disabled the child and removed him from the classroom.

Although not something I've experienced with three year old children, it is something I've dealt with in classes of older children. The common thread - the excuses made by the parents and the denial that they all hide-behind!!!

Making Excuses:

In today's society it seems that "blaming" others is all too common a practice. For example, the mother who is trying to teach responsibility and accountability to her son is blamed by the child and school for his being "tardy" to school because he didn't respond to the alarm or her repeated attempts to "wake" the child in a timely manner.

The government and banks blame the homeowner that can no longer afford his/her house payments and who has exhausted their six month or more reserves worth of savings to make ends meet for being irresponsible and getting into debt over their head instead of looking at the "real" culprit for the economic hardship(s) suffered by the family or the fact that they'd HAD a reserve from which to pull funds.

The problem with making excuses for and giving explanations for a child's misbehavior(s) is that it doesn't "help" the child. It doesn't HELP anybody. In fact, it does nothing but cloud one's judgment preventing any form of objective observation from being made thereby eliminating any real assistance being implemented.

Children, like adults, should be held accountable for their actions, decisions, and behaviors. Teaching children that they must learn to function within the established boundaries and to perform in a socially acceptable manner is the responsibility of his/her parents. It is a parent's job to teach him/her how to solve problems appropriately; they must be taught to interact socially. Above all else, when the child steps out of the realm of socially acceptable, the parent needs to "step up" instead of making one excuse after another.

What's Your Child's Excuse?

Apparently, the out-of-control child that I described above was under a new medication and therefore he was "acting out", according to his mother. Unfortunately, this type of behavior had been demonstrated throughout the school year and was not something that was attributable to a "new medication". This mother is and has been living in denial. The victim, her child, and perhaps someone else's child, should he not receive the necessary intervention and help that is needed.

Children, nor adults, should be able to blame others or make excuses because they were unable to or did not meet clearly defined expectations. By doing so, the only thing that we are encouraging is one's ability to place the blame or pass the buck instead of accepting the responsibility for his/her actions or lack thereof.

Making excuses or blaming others is something that will last a lifetime. The child who has had excuses made for him/her since childhood will very likely grow up following the same pattern making excuses for him or herself. Eventually the child for whom all of the excuses were made will have to be able to perform in life as an adult. The parent has ultimately disabled the adult to perform as a responsible adult. For instance, the teenager that was tardy nearly every day may ultimately grow up to be the employee that is late for work almost every day who offers an excuse as easy as he/she breathes. "There was an automobile accident"; "My son wouldn't get in the car so I could leave the house." or "I had to stop and get gas." The list of excuses goes on and on and the ultimate victim - the individual making them.

When parents make excuses for their children, it is typically the parent's inability to face the reality. The reality is that these parents are living in denial. It is easier to make an excuse or offer an explanation than to tackle the real problem(s). The sad reality is that the child is often the individual left suffering. Should the child actually have behavioral problems, learning disabilities or mental health issues, the constant outpouring of excuses and explanations will not provide him/her the necessary intervention(s) for teaching him/her to function appropriately. No matter what the diagnosis, a child will have to grow up and learn how to perform in an acceptable manner. Why place a stumbling block along their path?

Put another way, an adult suffering from Attention-Deficit-Hyperactive Disorder or Bipolar Disorder will have to function in society as an adult. They will be expected to get themselves out of bed and to work in order to earn an income to sustain life and its expenses. They will have to be able to perform and be productive in society. They won't be able to throw up their hands an offer the excuse or explanation "I'm ADHD and therefore cannot concentrate or complete my job responsibilities but I should still receive a paycheck!" This is where the "buck" stops!!!

The Alternative Response:

First and foremost let's address making excuses. Although annoying and disabling, it is not a sign of being a bad parent. It is extremely ineffective and will ultimately make parenting a much more difficult task. Recognizing that regardless of the child's problem(s), he/she will have to learn to deal with them in order to function as adults. Parents cannot "fix" or "solve" their child's problems, they must empower the child to do it themselves. The first step is to eliminate the excuses.

Once the excuses are eliminated from the equation, you can then handle the problem in a straightforward manner. For instance, instead of offering the excuse that a new medication is the reason your child threw a chair with the intent to hurt others and hit the teacher in the face, you address the exact behavior and identify a specific consequence for the specific behavior. Remember, consequences for inappropriate behaviors should be clearly understood by everyone before incidents occur and they result when poor choices are made not as a punishment for bad behavior. (For more information on consequences, please review my article Accountability and Consequences).

In the situation described at the beginning of this article, the parent of the child who'd exercised poor choices listened to her son as he clung to his mother whining about attending a classmate's party the next day while the teacher described his inappropriate actions. The parent should have explained that based on his efforts to harm not just (1) but several of his "friends" would prevent him from attending the classmate's birthday party. Being straightforward and to the point would have been the right path to take. This type of consequence would identify the inappropriate behavior and result in an appropriate consequence which would thereby eliminate the undesired, socially unacceptable behavior in which the child frequently engaged.

Note: Sadly, his mother made another "exception" for her child's behavior and the child was able to attend the child's party. Lesson learned: Do as I please!!!

Responsibility is the Solution:

Unfortunately, when parents and children focus on excuses and explanations, no one learns. Consequences are the ultimate key to teaching responsibility. When appropriate consequences are put into place, parents are able to shift the path of "excuse making" into a path of "meeting responsibilities."

It is a parenting strategy that must be implemented daily and one that some parent's will find time-consuming and difficult as it will be met with arguing, debates and even the "silent" treatment. If I may use the phrase, "Man up" because you're going to have to break the cycle that you began. Parents are the single-most influential person in a child's attitude, behaviors, and level of responsibility or lack thereof.

Change = Accountability for basic responsibility. Consequences reinforce responsible behaviors.

CHAPTER SIX

WHAT BEGINS WITH THE LETTER "F"?

Family Fun Activities

With the hustle and bustle of everyday life, family time seems to be pushed aside while mom prepares dinner, dad mows the lawn, and the kids finish their homework and prepare for some type of meeting or practice. Chances are, while these activities are taking place, the television is blasting in at least one room of your home. It is unusual if "communication" in the form of conversation is occurring and more likely than not it is in the form of "hurry up", "finish your homework" or "we're running late.

Families no longer resemble the traditional model. Now, don't get me wrong, I do enjoy the conveniences of indoor plumbing, heat at the touch of a button and being able to run to the grocery store via automobile whenever I need something. Change is good, but only to a point. What I'm referring to is more along the lines of the time spent at the meal table engaged in meaningful conversation with the television turned OFF (imagine that), being able to talk to your children WITHOUT headphones blasting music into their ears, and perhaps enjoying a game that doesn't require electricity, batteries or wires. You know, the simpler way of life.

Last year, I realized that I was falling into the family lifestyle and pattern of chaos that many people are they, too, have slipped into. I recognized that although I once knew my children very well, I really didn't know them anymore. Yes, they were quickly becoming teenagers and desired privacy while enjoying their independence, but that didn't mean that I suddenly had to take a backseat and watch from afar. I decided to make a change in an effort to re-establish or improve lines of communication through modifying certain areas of our daily lives.

I created a list of the things I'd enjoyed most when my children were younger and what I discovered was that it was the simplest things in life. Sitting down and playing cards and board games, reading a book together, having a "real" conversation, eating all of our meals

together at the table, taking walks in the park or on the beach, going on a bike ride or just hanging out in the backyard. I continued to expand upon my list of good memories to include activities away from home like visiting the zoo or a museum, traveling to another city, state or country to "sight-see" and enjoy the culture, participation in community activities and simply spending time together doing things that were unfamiliar, yet new to us. At that moment it hit me. Although I couldn't relive the past as my children were no longer toddlers or even elementary aged children, I could include some of the activities that we'd once enjoyed as a family that teenagers would still find enjoyable as well as create new opportunities for family time and growth.

I began by "cutting back" on extra-curricular activities as these really took a large portion of our "family time" on a daily basis. For example, when my boys participated in a local swim team, they were required to attend practice (4) afternoons per week. Practice began at 4:30 p.m. and ended at 6:30 p.m. This did not take into consideration getting changed into dry clothes, travel time of thirty minutes both to and from practice, the fact that they still needed to complete their homework, and any time for "free time". This one activity consumed twelve hours or more a week of our "family time". It led to tension between mom and children as they would be starving when practice was finished and extremely impatient regarding dinner preparation and meal time. They were too tired to apply themselves to their schoolwork and most importantly, "closed off" from any type of family activity or conversation. Because we were committed to the team, we completed the season and then focused our time and energy on activities less time consuming.

We found activities that the boys were interested in participating but which didn't involve traveling across town, occurred immediately after school and still allowed the boys enough "free time" during the course of the week so they were able to enjoy their lives. Their grades no longer suffered from their exhaustion and inability or desire to want to complete it and we were able to eat dinner as a family at a decent hour. By eliminating such a "time killer" we were able to focus on family fun activities and re-build our family.

I decided that we'd purchase a *Ping Pong table* for the family for Christmas that year. What a wonderful gift as it has been a focal point in our family fun. We have tournaments, enjoy practicing and just hanging out playing together. It is perfect when the boys have friends come over as it allows them to be interactive **WITHOUT** being glued to a television or gaming system. I also purchased a *dart board*. Again, a perfect "game" or "activity" that is better suited to teenage boys and enjoyable for the entire family. Like many families these days, we have gaming systems. The one that really is enjoyed by the "family" is the Wii system. Mom, dad, cousins, aunts and all of their friends have enjoyed this *interactive activity.* Yes, it is a video game but one that involves the entire body and not just the thumbs and fingers. It allows us to play together (up to four players) and really enjoy ourselves while challenging one another to a game of bowling, tennis, golf or even dancing.

Our family fun modifications didn't end there. I'd purchased a *trampoline (enclosed variety)* the year before which had seen hours upon hours of kids jumping, flipping and just having a great time. Even though it was still being used, it wasn't as entertaining as it had once been UNTIL we moved the basketball goal within reach. It was like a brand new activity had been invented. The boys, and their friends, were on the trampoline all over again as they could dunk the basketball, throw a football into the hoop while still practicing their awesome tricks. Even mom could participate from time to time. Whether we are on the trampoline or just watching, we are able to engage in conversation and share this time together.

Another modification was creating a "Game Night" each week in which we play board games or cards as a family. It has been a lot of fun as there are a lot of really fun games on the market these days. Some are strategic in nature while others are a combination of strategy and just plain fun. A few that we'd recommend to someone interested in establishing a game night for their families would include:

- Cadoo
- Cranium
- Upwords
- The Game of Things
- Words of WizDumb
- Don't Make Me Laugh
- Catch Phrase

We've also enjoyed some of the more traditional board games that have been around for quite some time as there is nothing wrong with integrating the old with the new. For example:

- Scrabble

- Monopoly
- Jenga (Extreme)
- Othello
- Chess
- Checkers
- Mancala
- Backgammon
- Cribbage
- Disney's Trivia 2

A few card games have made it into game night and include:

- Spades
- Hearts
- Rummy; and as the children have gotten older
- Poker

Each of these games has allowed us to spend at least 2 hours of uninterrupted, quality family time each week. We usually play right after dinner while still at the table. To make the time even more rewarding, I allow the boys to choose what we'll eat for dinner that evening followed by a dessert of their choice as well.

This simple modification and inclusion into our weekly routine has provided us a wonderful opportunity to re-connect with our teenagers and enjoy an activity while strengthening our family bond. This is not to say that it's always "peachy" as sometimes attitudes present themselves as nobody in our family likes to lose. But, the positive moments outweigh the moments we'd rather avoid.

I'll discuss other Family Fun Activities in future topics including, *Vacationing with Children*. Please read, enjoy and hopefully implement some of the ideas that will help you build a stronger family.

Are Four Wheelers Safe for Children?

Being raised in a family of four girls, it was a whole new ballgame when I gave birth to two sons. The differences started early on as they preferred baseballs and bicycles over dolls and ballet lessons. For me it was a new adventure, and quite a scary one. Trying to recognize and internalize the fact that boys are naturally rough and tumble was probably the most difficult lesson I'd ever had to learn. Learning to loosen the "umbilical" cord and allow them freedom to do what little boys desire to do was frustrating as all I wanted to do was protect and prevent them from getting hurt.

Over the years, I've learned that as a mom, you just have to let go (to a certain degree). They're going to hurt themselves and each other but apparently that's the name of the game for brothers and boys (as long as hurting the other isn't intentional). Thankfully, my boys are equally matched in size and strength so I don't have to worry quite as much as perhaps boys who aren't paired quite as equally. But that doesn't mean I don't worry.

These days, entertainment extends beyond the back yard, tree houses, and sling shots. It encompasses so many activities that can be deemed dangerous and that ARE actually quite dangerous. Determining what activities that you're going to allow your children to engage should be taken seriously as many children are injured and killed each year participating in activities that aren't safe and/or properly supervised. Although there are many, and I'm not going to cover each of them. I want to address one in particular as over 40,000 children are *injured and/or killed annually* as they engage in riding four-wheelers.

Four-wheelers aren't toys!!! This is the first concept that every parent and/or adult needs to understand. They are vehicles that can operate at speeds of up to 80 miles per hour. On top of that, they aren't equipped with seat belts, doors, sides, airbags, a roll cage or anything to keep the occupants, whether child or adult, from being ejected from the vehicle. I suppose the first question a parent should ask themselves, when considering purchasing a four-wheeler for their child or children is, "Would I allow my eight, ten, twelve or fourteen year old to drive my vehicle?" If you answered "no", you may want to rethink your decision about allowing them to drive and/or ride along on a four-wheeler then.

As often is the case, the most seriously injured individual in a motor vehicle accident isn't the driver but the passenger - especially in the case of four-wheeler accidents. This is because passengers have little to hold onto. Now consider the fact that most four-wheelers are being driven on rough terrain, off-road, more often on uneven surfaces than not, and typically in areas with very little if no visibility by adult(s), you can probably understand how this vehicle and the environment in which it is used provide a substantial potential for disaster. In fact, it isn't necessarily a passenger becoming injured or killed when these vehicles collide with or flip, but instead simply being thrown off due to the four-wheeler traveling too fast or being driven too fast over bumps or through ditches.

As mentioned above, 40,000 injuries or deaths have been attributed to four-wheelers annually just in the United States alone. It has become such an epidemic that the **American Academy of Pediatrics and the American Academy of Orthopedic Surgeons** have recommended and adopted policies stating that children under the age of 16 years not drive all-terrain vehicles or more specifically, four-wheelers. Some states have gotten more specific in their recommendations and laws including Texas who adopted laws regulating the use of four-wheelers and included that drivers under the age of 14 must be supervised by an adult at all times; and that all drivers and riders MUST wear a helmet and eye protection. Additionally, anyone operating or riding on ATV's must take an all-terrain safety course. Unfortunately, many people ignore the laws and the end result is often one that could have been avoided.

One of the most predominate problems in the U.S. regarding ATV's is that parents will often purchase (1) vehicle that will be driven by all the members of the family regardless of their size. What this does is create an unsafe situation right from the start. If a child isn't large enough to straddle the ATV comfortably, they've virtually had one source of stability taken away from them before the vehicle even begins to move.

Children under the age of six should NEVER be allowed on a four-wheeler. It simply isn't safe for them. Unfortunately, parents will often cave in to the demands of their screaming, pleading child who desires to ride along with other family members. Many times, they've been known to start and ride the ATV without the permission of anyone if given the opportunity - unsupervised. Additionally, children will often experience the "thrill" of riding an ATV when visiting friends - unbeknownst to parents. This experience, while fun for the child, may also prove tragic.

If you are considering purchasing an ATV for the entertainment of your children, please reconsider. Too many things can happen that may haunt you and/or your child forever. There are safer, more appropriate forms of entertainment that are intended for children.

Please consider these tips & suggestions before blindly sending your child off to someone else's home (trust me, it happens):

- **<u>Get to know your Neighbors (or child's friend's family)</u>** - Believe it or not, people aren't always what they may seem. Some families operate under a totally different set of acceptable and unacceptable standards than you may. Case & Point: One of my son's friend's parents found it perfectly acceptable for their son (age 12) to ride both a motorbike and an ATV whenever he chose without parental supervision. This was not something that I condone and immediately had to establish a rule with both the parents of the child and the child that under NO circumstance would my son be allowed to engage in these activities.

- **<u>Establish Rules (at home and away) for your Child</u>** - Make certain that your child understands your rules and which they may NOT violate when visiting others. I know, rules are meant to be broken, or so some individuals believe, but safety and well-being of your child is the most important issue and explaining to them that, although these activities appear to be fun, they are also extremely dangerous. I would recommend allowing your child to view safety videos and footage of accidents so that they fully comprehend the dangers associated with ATV's.

- **<u>Choose Appropriately Sized ATV's</u>** - Although as you've probably deduced by now, I am not a proponent of ATV's. I've witnessed fatal accidents which could have been prevented and seen "children" operating vehicles that they couldn't control. If you are of the opposing opinion and decide that this is a form of entertainment that you'd like to provide your family, choose ATV's that will fit the members of the family. If you intend to allow younger children to operate and/or ride as a passenger, choose an ATV that will "fit" them. The same is true for older drivers/passengers in your family. One-size-does NOT fit all when it comes to ATV's.

- **<u>Provide Safety and Equipment</u>** - If providing your family with the opportunity to operate or ride an ATV, invest in training. There are safety courses available that anyone intending to drive or ride should engage. Additionally, ensure that each member of your family who will be riding has properly fitted helmets and goggles. These pieces of equipment are intended to provide a certain element of protection and definitely worth the expense. If you can afford an ATV you can afford the necessities. ATV Safety courses are available online. For information on Safety Courses, please visit http://www.atvsafety.org/

With summer here and parents looking for ways to provide entertainment for their children, it isn't uncommon for decisions to be made without weighing all of the facts. Please consider your decision to purchase a four-wheeler or other ATV carefully and make certain that you take the necessary precautions before doing so. Most of all remember, you wouldn't make a hasty decision about the type of vehicle to purchase or allow your teenage driver to operate would you?

CHAPTER SEVEN

WHAT BEGINS WITH THE LETTER "G"?

Hidden Sources of Gluten

Last week, after researching and writing an article entitled *Gluten-Free, Casein-Free Diet as a Treatment for Autism* and reporting some of the findings associated with the careful modification and monitoring of foods consumed by autistic children, I promised that I'd be preparing a list of foods containing gluten which I believe will be helpful in determining what things you should be avoiding in your everyday experiences and diet in order to help your autistic child. You'll be very surprised what I discovered about common, everyday products containing gluten.

What I discovered is that GLUTEN is everywhere. Not only is it in the foods that we eat but it can be found is many cosmetic & hygiene products, household products and just plain everyday products that parents wouldn't think to consider when attempting to eliminate Gluten from their child's diet. So, without further ado, let me provide you the shocking list of *"Gluten Containing Products"*:

1. *Lipstick & lip balm* contain Gluten. So moms, be careful when "kissing" that precious child on the lips. You might want to modify the items your child uses when playing "dress-up" as no longer is decorating his/her face with lipstick a good idea in a gluten-free lifestyle. **NOTE: BURT'S BEESWAX LIP BALM IS GLUTEN-FREE**.

2. *Sunscreen.* Please don't let it deter you from protecting your child's skin from the harmful effects of the sun. NOTE: **BANANA BOAT CHILDRENS SUNSCREEN IS GLUTEN-FREE.**

3. *Certain medications and antibiotics* contain Gluten. If you've chosen to provide your child a Gluten-Free Lifestyle, you'll need to check with both your doctor and pharmacist about medications (topical & oral) that will be Gluten-Free.

4. *Stamps & Envelopes* both contain Gluten in the sticking adhesive. If you intend to allow your child assist with this simple household task, it would be wise to

purchase envelopes that have a removable backing and stamps as well. (In other words, no licking and sticking by your child).

5. *Ground Spices* used for cooking. NOTE: **McCormick BRAND SPICES ARE 100% PURE SPICE.**

6. *Toothpaste and Mouthwashes* contain Gluten. NOTE: **TOM'S OF MAINE PROVIDE GLUTEN-FREE DENTAL CARE PRODUCTS.**

7. *Laundry detergent(s)* contain Gluten. NOTE: **ARM & HAMMER BAKING SODA DETERGENT IS GLUTEN- FREE.**

8. *Children's Stickers*, like envelopes & stamps, contain Gluten. This also includes stickers such as price tags.

9. *Cosmetics* such as foundations, liquid blushes, etc...contain Gluten. Again, avoidance of these basic products found at home will require special storage and handling.

10. *Soaps & Shampoos*. You and your child will not have to sacrifice good hygiene. NOTE: **KIRKMAN LAB'S KLEEN products are available in Gluten-Free formulas**.

11. Last but not least, and perhaps an area that you wouldn't think to include in a Gluten-Free lifestyle should be in the use of *Household Appliances*. For example, toasters, ovens, microwaves, waffle irons, etc... In order to eliminate the chance of your autistic child being exposed to Gluten, you'll need to use separate utensils for Gluten-Free foods. Additionally, when cooking or reheating foods within an oven or microwave, you'll want to place Gluten-Free, Casein-Free foods on a plate.

Now that we've addressed common everyday household products containing Gluten, lets address the food items and additives common in our daily diets that will need to be eliminated altogether if your plans to provide a *Gluten-Free, Casein-Free* are to be effective. These lists are quite extensive and remember you'll want to always review labels when shopping for foods for your child. It might even be a good idea to print this list to carry along with you when you are shopping for groceries. Below is a list of:

Unsafe Additives & Ingredients found in raw form & processed foods which contain Gluten & Casein proteins:

- Abyssinian Hard (Wheat Triticum duran)
- Acidophilus Milk

- Alcohol (Spirits - Certain Varieties)
- Artificial Butter flavoring (check your cooking sprays, Crisco Butter, I Can't Believe it's Not Butter)
- Aspartame (can cause IBS symptoms - and is found in LOTS of foods, candies, gum.
- Avena
- Baking Powder & Soda (again, verify brand & specific ingredients)
- Barley
- Barley Malt
- Barley Hordeum Vulgare
- Beer
- Bleached All-Purpose Flour
- Bouillon Cubes or Powder
- Bran
- Bulgur (Bulgur Wheat/Nuts)
- Butter
- Butter Fat
- Butter Flavoring
- Butter Oil
- Buttermilk
- Bran
- Broth Prepackaged
- Calcium Caseinate
- Caramel Color
- Casein
- Caseinates
- Cheese (Hard or Soft)
- Cereal Extract
- Cereal Binding
- Chilton
- Chorizo (read label)
- Coffee Creamer Substitute (grain based)
- Cottage Cheese
- Cream Yogurt
- Croutons

- Custard
- Curds
- Delactosed whey
- Demineralized whey
- Dextrin
- Durum
- Edible Starch
- Farina
- Filler
- Gelatinized Starch
- Glutamate (Free)
- Glutamic Acid
- Gravy Cubes
- Gravy Mixes (unless homemade with cornstarch)
- Ground Spices (excluding McCormick Brand which are Gluten-Free)
- Gum Base
- Half & Half
- Hard Wheat
- Herbs with Wheat Fillers
- Hydrolysates: Casein
- Hordeum
- Hydrolyzed Oat Starch
- Hydrolyzed Plant Protein (HPP)
- Hydrolyzed Vegetable Protein (HVP)
- Job's Tears (aka Pearl Barley)
- Kamut (Pasta Wheat)
- Lactoglobulin
- Lactose
- Lactalbumin
- Lactalbumin Phosphate
- Magnesium Caseinate
- Malt
- Malt Extract
- Malt Flavoring
- Malt Syrup

- Malt Vinegar
- Miso
- Modified Food Starch (source is either corn or wheat)
- Modified Starch
- MSG (Manufactured Outside USA)
- Mustard Powder (verify labels as some contain Gluten)
- Natural Flavoring
- White Grain Vinegar
- White Vinegar

****Please Note: Lactic Acid is often listed on a product label as an ingredient as it is commercially produced from whey, cornstarch, potatoes and molasses. Always verify its source. ****

The following is a list of flours that you will need to avoid in a GFCF diet:

- Barley Flour
- Bleached All-Purpose Flour
- Bread Flour
- Brown Flour
- Durum Flour
- Einkorn Wheat
- Enriched Flour
- Fu (Dried Wheat Gluten)
- Galactose
- Germ
- Gluten Flour
- Graham Flour
- Granary Flour
- High Protein Flour
- High Gluten Flour
- Job's Tears (aka Pearl Barley)
- Kamut (Pasta Wheat)
- Oat Flour
- Oats
- Pasta

- Pearl Barley
- Potassium Caseinate
- Prepackaged Sauce Mixes (read labels carefully - most contain wheat)
- Rice Malt (contains barley or Koji)
- Rice Syrup (unless the label indicates Gluten-Free, it contains barley enzymes)
- Rye
- Rye Semolina
- Seiten
- Semolina
- Semolina Triticum
- Scotch (not that you'll be feeding this to your child - but autistic adults should avoid)
- Shoyu (soy sauce)
- Small Spelt
- Soba Noodles
- Sodium Caseinate (contains MSG)
- Sodium Lactylate (may or may not contain casein - read label carefully)
- Soy Sauce (unless label indicates Gluten-Free)
- Spirits (read the labels)
- Spelt
- Spelt Triticum Spelta
- Spices with Wheat Fillers
- Starch (manufactured outside the USA)
- Stativa
- Stock Cubes (many contain Gluten)
- Strong Flour
- Suet in Packets
- Sulfites
- Teriyaki Sauce
- Tritical
- Triticale X triticosecale
- Triticum
- Udon (Wheat Noodles)
- Vegetable Starch
- Vital Gluten

- Vitamins (some contain Gluten)
- Vulgar
- Wheat
- Wheat Bran
- Wheat Durum Triticum
- Wheat Flour
- Wheat Germ
- Wheat Gluten
- Wheat Malt
- Wheat Nuts
- Wheat Oats
- Wheat Pasta
- Wheat Starch
- Wheat Triticum Aestivum
- Wheat Triticum Mononoccum
- Whey
- Whey Protein
- Whey Protein Concentrate
- Whey Sodium Caseinate
- White Flour
- Whole-Meal Flour
- Whole Wheat Berries

The following milk, milk products and ingredients containing milk protein flavorings will also need to be eliminated from your child's GFCF diet:

- Bavarian Cream Flavoring
- Brown Sugar Flavoring
- Butter Milk
- Caramel Coloring
- Coconut Cream Flavoring
- Condensed Milk
- Dry Milk
- Evaporated Milk
- Goat's Milk

- Half & Half
- Low Fat Milk Fat
- Malted Milk
- Milk Cheese Lactose
- Milk Derivatives
- Milk Powder
- Milk Solids
- Non-Dairy Butter
- Non-Dairy Creamer
- Pudding
- Rennet Casein
- Sour Cream
- Sour Cream Solids
- Sour Milk Solids
- Whey (in all forms including sweet, delectated, protein concentrate)
- Yogurt

NOTE: Luncheon meats, hotdogs and sausages MAY contain milk protein so ALWAYS check the labels.

A quick reference guide of definite "NO NO" foods which contain wheat & flour include:

- Biscuits
- Bread
- Bread Crumbs
- Cake Flour
- Cake & Cake Mixes
- Chow Mein Noodles
- Coffee Creamer (any kind)
- Cookies
- Cookie Mixes
- Crackers
- Croutons
- Doughnuts
- Flavored Instant Coffee

- Flavored Instant Tea
- Flavored Prepackaged Pasta
- Flavored Prepackaged Rice
- Flour Tortillas
- Ice Cream Cones
- Pasta
- Pizza
- Prepackaged Hot Chocolate
- Prepackaged Snack Cakes
- Pretzels

The good news is that most of these food items can now be purchased both *Gluten & Casein Free.* Sometimes they can be found at your local grocery store chains, other times you may be required to check at a Health Food Store or in Natural Food Stores. If all else fails, you can utilize resources found online.

For additional information on purchasing *Gluten-Free & Casein-Free Foods* online, visit http://www.glutensolutions.com, or you can visit

http://www.celiac.com/catalog/product_info.php?products_id=181.

Preventing your child from eating foods or coming into contact with products that contain either Gluten & Casein will be an enormous task as so many things contain one, the other or both but the payoff, should it prove effective, will be well worth your effort.

In order to ensure that the foods you purchase are **GFCF** will be time consuming and somewhat frustrating. The frustration can be reduced if you create a two week menu that encompasses all meals (including snacks) that you can use repetitively over the course of the "trial" period which adheres to the dietary restrictions above. Always remember, even though this list is thorough, you should verify EACH of the ingredients on labels of products your purchase.

If you discover that your child is benefitting from the modification(s) to his/her diet through the elimination of Gluten & Casein, you may choose to prepare his/her meals from scratch vs prepackaged **GFCF** foods. There are <u>Gluten-Free, Casein-Free Cookbooks</u> available with tasty recipes that you and your entire family can enjoy.

For additional information regarding cooking **GFCF** foods, you can visit Chef Tom Dickinson of Red Kitchen Food Company:

http://www.myspace.com/redkitchenfoodcompany

I wish you and your child much success.

CHAPTER EIGHT

WHAT BEGINS WITH THE LETTER "H"?

Healthy Eating Habits

Healthy snacking and eating habits begin at an early age. In fact, it begins as early as your child's toddler years. It isn't the toddler that chooses or prepares his/her snacks and meals but up to the caregiver whether that is mom, dad, Grandma or the babysitter.

Establishing acceptable eating standards is up to you as a parent and should begin immediately after the birth of your child, if not before. Ensuring that anyone who will be responsible for **providing meals/snacks** to your child should be aware of what you prefer and elect not to serve. For example, making certain that the babysitter understands that the Movie Theater Microwave Popcorn in the pantry is for Bridge Night only and that the Organic Dehydrated Banana Bites or the fresh applesauce in the refrigerator is a snack for your child.

Healthy eating habits for your children should realistically be shared by everyone in the home especially since it is common knowledge that children learn through observation and modeling of behaviors, even eating habits. Did you know that research has suggested that children who are taught to eat healthy foods such as fruits and vegetables instead of chips and cookies will choose the healthier foods over the less healthy foods more often than not? These healthy eating choices will prevail throughout your child's lifetime if they begin early and are practiced consistently.

Wouldn't it be nice to have your 7, 10, 13 or even 16 year old preferring a home prepared meal over fast foods? I thought it would so I took the necessary steps to ensure healthy eating habits by my two sons, now ages 19 and 21. Although it wasn't always easy, I prepared their baby foods from organic fruits, vegetables and meats (prepared the night before along with our evening meal) from the day they ate their first "real" foods. In fact, my sons didn't visit a "fast food" restaurant until we traveled across country when my boys were aged 3-1/2 and 5 and restaurants serving healthier meals weren't readily available. Even then, I opted for beans and rice options over meat or what was supposed to be meat. They didn't even taste a soft drink until they attended school and beverages of this type were served at parties.

Planning a weekly menu and sticking to it is the first step in not only establishing good eating habits for you and your family, but also saving money that might otherwise be wasted eating in restaurants and throwing away foods that aren't consumed because something else came up that prevented you from cooking. By planning your menu, you are able to shop accordingly, saving money, and plan your child's meal in advance which means being organized enough to prepare the necessary ingredients for their meals ahead of time.

At first it might seem tedious, but it becomes second nature in about three weeks. And, just think of the savings. My oldest son's appetite would have required my taking out a second mortgage if I'd relied on prepackaged baby foods. Instead, I was able to prepare his foods from the ingredients used preparing meals for my husband and me. Once calculated, my savings was approximately $36.00 per week when comparing the cost of home prepared organic fruits, grains and vegetables to the prepackaged and prepared organic foods of the same variety and quantity.

To this day, I still prepare their lunches and dinners, even though my schedule is hectic as I work outside the home, and am responsible for transporting them to sporting events and practices. I feel that my due diligence has paid off as I observe my children choosing an orange over a cookie, and watch them enjoying their vegetables with their evening meals. I've never been the parent apologizing for my child's refusal to eat the meal that is served nor had to deal with them electing to go without eating. Additionally, I've never been the "short order cook" at home attempting to prepare something for each individual due to my children having developed finicky eating habits. My sons are both physically healthy; do not suffer from acne resulting from excessive sugars or salts or poor nutrition in general nor do they struggle with being overweight.

Healthy eating habits will play an important role in the overall health of your child. Why not give your children a "head-start" by teaching (modeling) ***healthy eating*** and providing the intellectual tools to make the right choices for a lifetime. You'll be glad you did.....and so will they.

Playing Sports & Staying Hydrated

1, 2, 3 - Kick 'em in the Knee..... (Just kidding - I remembered that from my childhood).

It's back to school and for many that means the sports season is underway. Whether your child plays football, soccer, baseball, plays in the marching band or is a cheerleader or drill-team member, it means *that proper hydration is necessary* to prevent health related issues from occurring.

For those of us in the south, temperatures range anywhere from the low to upper 90's and this can lead to serious heat related issues without the addition of uniforms, pads, etc. When you factor in these protective measures, you're literally increasing the body's temperature by another 5 or more degree.

Proper hydration is KEY!!!

Temperature & Hydration Considerations:

Parents should always consider the temperature when allowing or even encouraging their children to play outside. We want children to participate in outdoor activities instead of remaining inside the house in front of the television or playing video games, but perhaps outdoor activities can be enjoyed by choosing times of the day, such as earlier in the morning or later in the afternoon, avoiding times when it is hottest outside such as in the middle of the day.

Now that our children are back in school or soon will be, our concern should be about heat exhaustion and heat stroke which often result during physical education courses and playing and/or participating in sports and athletics. I have always made it a point to emphasize the *importance of maintaining hydration.* I encourage my children to drink a glass of water in between the consumption of other beverages that they consume and I try to choose beverages that aren't loaded with sugar, contain no caffeine and/or artificial sweeteners.

How serious is it?

Between the years 1999 - 2003, The Centers for Disease Control and Prevention reported a total of 3,442 heat and exposure related (elevated body temperatures) deaths. Of these, 7% or 242 were children under the age of 15 years. These statistics may not seem alarming although if your child was among one of them I think you'd feel differently.

In fact, among high school athletes, heat stroke from exertion is the third leading cause of death and is often related to a child's unfamiliarity with and/or not being properly acclimated to the heat. Throw in the child's lack of hydration and you've got a serious situation on hand.

What is Heat Exhaustion?

Heat exhaustion occurs when the core body temperature is elevated between 100.4 and 104 degrees. This is accomplished quite easily without proper hydration and with the addition of padding and safety equipment.

Although the symptoms are typically non-specific they can include **_muscle cramps, fatigue, thirst, nausea, vomiting and headaches_**. The skin is usually cool and moist from sweating which is indicative that the body's cooling mechanism is working. The pulse rate is rapid and weak and breathing is fast and shallow. At this point, serious health issues can evolve including death. It is important to know what to do to prevent further escalation of any kind.

What to do if you suspect Heat Exhaustion:

The first thing that should be done in the form of treatment is to move the victim to a cooler place such as to a spot in the shade, into an air conditioned room, etc... to prevent the natural progression to heat stroke. Immediately try to make the individual comfortable by removing as much clothing as possible (uniforms, pads, helmets etc...) to help the heat dissipation more quickly. Lightly mist the individual with water to cool the body's temperature from the outside and immediately begin re-hydration with the appropriate oral electrolyte solutions and water. Avoid using salt tablets or potassium tablets for hydration purposes as these aren't healthy.

It is better to use sports drinks diluted with water as sports drinks typically contain more sugar than necessary or recommended. Additionally, eating a banana, an orange, carrot or even a sports bar will replace the body's electrolytes and potassium in a healthier manner. When choosing sports drinks, read the labels carefully as you may not be getting what you bargained for. Many drinks contain artificial sweeteners which can affect children in many ways - for more information on artificial sweeteners, please read my articles, Sweetened to Death!!! (Aspartame) or All Sweeteners are NOT the Same (Sucralose). Finally, simply drinking water is not enough as it doesn't provide the sodium necessary in the diet.

There are many products on the market for hydration and providing the necessary electrolytes that a body needs when exerting itself. Let's first identify WHAT we're trying to replenish and why.

Electrolytes are minerals like sodium, potassium and chloride that help balance blood acidity. They are lost in sweat, which is why sweat tastes salty. Our bodies have plenty of electrolytes. Salt, for example, is usually eaten in great excess. In order to provide the proper balance, many "sports drinks" and "additives" have been marketed to do just that. But remember, you can also eat properly to gain the necessary minerals that one's body needs.

Excellent Electrolyte Beverages & Fruits & Vegetables:

- Gatorade Orange Sports Drink; 10 - 32 oz. bottles - $18.90
- Powerade Ion 4; 6 - 32 oz. - $11.95
- Vitamin Water; 12 - 20 oz. - $28.74
- Sustain Sport On-the-Go; 20 packets - $10.99. Visit www.AdvocareNation.us and complete the contact sheet with your inquiry for details (my own children use this product).
- EMERGEN-C ELECTRO MIX Lemon-Lime .1 oz. packet, 30 pk. per Box - $10.01
- Carrots
- Oranges or Orange Juice (diluted 1/3)
- Bananas
- Clif Bar Energy Bar, Carrot Cake - 24 pack $30.15

- <u>Nature's Path Organic Optimum Energy Bar - Pomegranate Cherry</u>; 12 - $15.38

When heat exhaustion is treated quickly and appropriately, symptoms usually resolve themselves within 20 -30 minutes. The child should not return to activities that day, and should avoid heat stress for several days.

What is Heat Stroke?

Heat stroke is a MEDICAL EMERGENCY and should not be taken lightly as the child(s) health and wellness is at critical risk. It will require transportation to the Emergency Room for aggressive treatment. When someone suffers from heat stroke, unfortunately the symptoms associated with heat exhaustion have either been missed or ignored and the core body temperature rises to 104 degrees or greater. The skin is flushed, hot and dry from a lack of sweating. The athlete will often appear confused, or may even be unconscious. The heart rate is fast and there is hyperventilation. The blood pools away from vital organs and can result in encephalopathy, liver, kidney and multiple organ failure. Does this sound serious enough??? Do not make matters worse by avoiding medical attention.

What You Can Do:

You can begin by being proactive with your children. Educating your children about the need for hydration the evening prior to events, as well as the need to continuously hydrate while exercising in the heat (or not) is imperative. They should understand that drinking fluids, even when they're not thirsty, is important as once they become thirsty they are more than likely already behind in their fluid intake.

Through proper health education and practices, and understanding and recognizing the early signs of heat exhaustion and overheating, many heat related illnesses and death are preventable.

Talk to your child's school about teaching students about heat exhaustion and the serious health illnesses that can result if the signs that our bodies provide are ignored. It is important that children are not made to feel "embarrassed", "less macho" or "belittled" for speaking up when they're feeling the effects from the heat.

As parents, form a co-op with other parents of athletes and alternate delivering sports drinks, fruits and water to the practices that often take place after school. This will ensure that your son or daughter has the means to prevent the unthinkable from occurring.

Also, remember who the adult is in this situation. If you feel that your child may become too distracted to stop and drink, perhaps showing up and providing a beverage to prevent dehydration is the solution.

CHAPTER NINE

WHAT BEGINS WITH THE LETTER "I"?

Talk to Your Kids about the Internet Safety and the World of Opportunities it May Provide

If you watch the news, read the paper or are involved in any form of social media you know the risks involved with the "internet" - they're virtually posted everywhere but not everyone takes the warnings to heart.

Children are the most vulnerable to the dangers online as they aren't always aware of the risks involved with social media, including but certainly not limited to chatting online, posting video and photo images from mobile devices and broadcasting to hundreds of people where they are or where they're going and what they'll be doing once they arrive. Talking to children about the risks involved, more or less an online etiquette, to protect them is necessary for all parents. If you have children with any form of mobile communication device, you may want to drop everything and have "the talk".

Many of us enjoy the world of opportunities that the internet provides. Whether it be in the form of personal entertainment and enjoyment or for business contacts, access and expansion, it is a wonderful tool. But, it doesn't come without risks - to adults too. For instance, on CBS Sunday Morning, a young teacher who'd posted photos on one of the social media platforms of her vacation abroad was forced to resign from her job as a teacher as a result of photos posted that showed her consuming alcoholic beverages. Fair, absolutely not. Did the school system have a valid point - yes they did. But, should anything and everything that we do be up for scrutiny? In the world of Facebook, Instagram and the other social media platforms, evidently it is.

Children are not aware of the risks involved with socializing and communicating online and via cellphone connections such as texting. Making our children aware of the following may help to reduce the risk of them falling victim to any sort of cyber-crime or social, emotional or physical harm:

- **Inappropriate Conduct** - Although we understand that there is always someone behind a message, contact, etc....online, children may feel that because they can't actually touch, see or hear the other side that it is anonymous. They need to understand that anything and everything that they do online - they'll ultimately be held accountable.

- **Inappropriate Contact** - Making children aware of the fact that not everyone online has good and/or appropriate intentions is paramount to their safety. Helping them understand that there will be bullies, predators (of many varieties), hackers and scammers who are just waiting the opportunity to find their next victim. Help make your children aware of these dangers explaining what might be lurking behind the monitor.

- **Inappropriate Context** - The internet has opened up an entirely new world filled with content that we'd prefer our children never be exposed. Unfortunately, it seems that often and no matter what precautions we put into place, they'll be exposed to content such as pornography, violence and perhaps hate speeches and references. You can certainly reduce these risks by communicating with your children and helping them recognize both the risks and precautions that they need to exercise to protect themselves.

Parents, reducing these risks can be as simple as talking to your children about how and with whom they communicate online. Not sure where to begin? Let me go over a few pointers.

- **Begin Early** - Children, even toddlers, are aware of and use electronic devices from time to time. So, as soon as your child or children begin using these types of devices independently, begin talking to them about safety and security. By addressing the topics early, you'll be able to teach them what's important and appropriate before someone else does.

- **Honesty is the Best Policy** - Children seek guidance from their parents and therefore it is up to us to be both supportive and positive. Children need to know that they can discuss topics with their parents and that their parents will listen attentively and take into account their feelings. Through "active" listening, children will be more likely to have meaningful conversations with you. Even though as parents we don't always have the answers, or perhaps we don't have the answers that they want to hear, being honest with our kids will certainly pave the way for continued communication.

- **Invite Conversations** - Sometimes children don't always feel comfortable initiating conversations - perhaps you're busy or preoccupied, perhaps the subject is something that isn't one that they feel overly excited about beginning - the solution....begin conversations with your children. Just like story-starters which encourage young students to write, you can use everyday situations to "strike-up" conversations with your children. Whether you use a scene from a television program and/or the news, make certain that you talk to your children about portrayals of real-life events so that they can be aware of the experiences others have fallen victim to and how they can protect themselves.

- **Share Your Values/Beliefs** - For the most part, parents raise their children according to a pre-established value system that they hold near and dear. Sometimes online situations seem to fall by the wayside if you don't clearly identify and explain what you believe and how it applies online. Again, communication is key - if you express to your children your expectations of their behavior online (and off) they'll be more likely to adhere to and make wiser decisions when and/if faced with unusual situations.

- **Be Patient** - As with anything in life, whether it is a sport, a new job or a subject in school, repetition is necessary in order for particular skills, concepts and behaviors to be learned. Patience will be necessary. Children (and some adults) need information to be presented multiple times before it actually sinks in which means that you'll have to be both persistent and patient. Trust me, in the long run; your patience will pay off.

With electronic media being increasingly present in our lives, and knowing that our children will ultimately be exposed to so many devices and opportunities for "foul-play", make certain that you talk to your children BEFORE it is too late. I cannot express the importance of communicating. Children spend eight or more hours at school per day communicating with their friends and countless additional hours of texting, chatting, playing video games and talking on the phone. Trust me when I say that these conversations often include topics of discussion that you'd prefer your children not engage.

Unfortunately, many children aren't raised by the same set of standards that you've established for your own children - if you don't believe me, just listen to the language being used when children are playing video games online or these days, via 360. It is enough to make you disconnect all devices and keep your children surrounded by guards. Realistically, we all know that this solution is no solution at all - but communicating, talking to and sharing your concerns, values, and establishing safety guidelines with your children are. Make sure you take the time to do it once, twice, and fifty times if needed. Eventually, your rules and safety measures will become ingrained and you'll be able to communicate regularly as needed.

Be sure to talk to your children - or someone else will!!!

CHAPTER TEN

WHAT BEGINS WITH THE LETTER "J"?

Top Ten Best Jobs for Teens

If your teens are anything like mine, I feel that I seriously need a second job just to fulfill the many expenses that go along with their hobbies, sports and/or social engagements.....Well, not anymore! It's high time they "get a job" and start contributing to their own needs.

Teenagers have many expenses that go along with both middle and high school related clubs and class projects, sports, after-sports events, hobbies and dating. Good grief - so many expenses.... so little budget.

Well, if you're venturing into these unknown waters (like me) you might consider allowing your son or daughter to begin working (on the side) to earn an income to help offset the many "unforeseen" expenses of raising a teen!

With the busy schedules that many teenagers have, and wanting them to keep their grades in tip-top shape, finding a job that works "with" them and their schedule is desirable. And, believe it or not, there are many suitable employment opportunities that will allow them to earn a buck or two and continue to excel in sports and school. So without further ado, let me outline the perfect jobs for you (teens)!

Top Ten Best Jobs for Teens:

- **Babysitting** - Now this is going to be more appealing to girls but let me just point out that its good money, good hours, and a comfortable environment (usually) and can be worked around YOUR own schedule. This opportunity is usually something that works best for teenagers between the ages of 13 and 18. The teen must be mature, responsible and have a nurturing/caring side. Babies and children can be difficult so patience is required. Downside: Changing Diapers, cleaning up vomit and perhaps trying to entertain them and stop them from crying. Perks: An opportunity to play with items that you've not played with in years; usually receive a free meal out of the deal; babies to cuddle; young children to snuggle; being looked up to by others; time to watch a movie or television along with them; opportunity (after bedtime) to complete homework assignments, etc...

- **Grocery Chains** - This opportunity may have age requirements, especially depending upon the specific job you are seeking. Jobs include stock clerks, bagging clerks, and cashiers. The pay is typically pretty decent for teens and grocery chains are more inclined to work around your sports schedules. Additionally, they'll usually include other teens with whom you can socialize and carpool if necessary. Two food stores that provide exceptional benefits, opportunities and coaching for teens are Publix and Ingles.

- **Retail Stores** - Although the hours may involve many during the weekends, it is a great job for teens. Retail stores provide an atmosphere where safety is pretty well covered. Flexible hours are a perk but you have to provide your schedule(s) in advance to allow for accommodating special engagements and/or events that you might have. Usually the pay is enough to fulfill that "pocket change" need that you've got.

- **Library** - Excellent opportunity for individuals who enjoy reading and BOOKS! The pay is usually acceptable (perhaps better), provide reasonable hours and also allow for a flexible schedule. It is the perfect atmosphere for individuals interested in learning about library management too.

- **Gardening/Landscape/Lawn Maintenance** - The perfect job to help out in and/or around your neighborhood. Many homeowners do not have the time to manage their lawns. They seek outside companies to mow, manicure and plant or perhaps even pull weeds. Often they'll have their own equipment that you can use, however, some may not. If this is a job you're interested in pursuing, distributing flyers within your community and/or posting bulletins at your local grocery store, church, etc....will often bring you the business. You'll want to discuss the equipment that is available and/or make certain that you've got your own and a way to transport it to and from the location.

- **Waiter/Waitress** - This can be a very challenging job but many teens really enjoy the experience. It takes a great deal of patience, excellent listening skills, and the ability to communicate effectively with others. Although the pay can be excellent, you'll often get stiffed if you're relying on tips as the major portion of your salary. Hotels generally pay anywhere from $9.00 to $12.00 per hour and include tips while local independently owned restaurants pay less and rely more heavily on tips. Fast food chains typically stick to minimum wage with slight raises over time. One restaurant that I can recommend is Chick-Fil-A as it is an excellent employer for teenagers.

- **Pet Sitting** - Another entrepreneurial job for teens and one that requires a love of pets. This job opportunity can be carried out within your neighborhood and/or community as long as you've got transportation. You must be honest and trustworthy, responsible, and enjoy animals. An excellent job that you can work around your schedule and they designated schedule of the pets. Fees can range anywhere from $20.00 to $65.00 dollars per visit depending upon the type and number of pets. Fish, birds and hamsters (or other furry friends) may allocate $20.00 per visit, while cats and dogs typically range $25 - $30.00 dollars per visit and include cleaning litter boxes, walking and feeding pet. Large animals such as farm animals, horses, etc....typically receive $65.00 or more dollars per visit. (It is NOT recommended that teens with NO experience around pets and especially large animals such as horses, farm animals, etc...take on this responsibility).

- **Tutoring** - If you are an "A" student and can work responsibly tutoring others (focusing on the studies at hand and not socializing and gabbing), you may be in a position to earn some extra cash. Many students struggle academically and need assistance. Often times, parents must seek outside resources to assist their children. These services may include testing fees, assessments, etc....and can be quite costly. If you are able to communicate effectively and assist others in specific academic areas, you might be just the person for the job. You, based upon your successes, can probably earn between $15 - $20 dollars per session, and the sessions should not exceed 1 hour.

- **Washing Cars** - This is a job that anyone can do. It can be done at local businesses (with the permission of the business owner) or at the home of the individual seeking your services. If they provide the water and supplies, you'll want to charge a specific rate (not by the hour) as this is something that can deter repeat business if you take too long. If the job includes waxing and polishing, vacuuming and more, consider (perhaps by practicing on a family member's vehicle to determine the time involved) how long each service will take and come up with a fee based on time involved. A full detail of a vehicle, both inside and out, typically range anywhere from $75.00 to $250.00 depending on the size and type of vehicle. Vinyl interiors /

leather interior and cloth interiors will require different types of treatments and can be labor intensive. Waxing as well. SUV's vs. compact cars really can make a time difference. Plan accordingly and have a "price chart" on hand.

- **Pool Cleaning** - This is a job that requires use of the swimming pool pretty much year round, so if you live in an area where swimming pools in everyone's back yard is prevalent, or perhaps a community pool, this might be the perfect opportunity for a teenager desiring to earn some spending money. Like car washing, you'll want to consider the different types of services that you'll be offering. Simply vacuuming and skimming the water surface; cleaning around the pool (plants, deck, or concrete surface); chemical treatment; covering; etc....Who knew there was so much to do with a swimming pool BEFORE you could swim in it? Determine the charges by calling local pool cleaning and maintenance companies to find what they usually charge. You'll want to charge less - unless you come with all of the resources, tools and perks that they can offer. NOTE: If you are NOT a swimmer and do not know the basic rules about what to do if you fall into a pool, this is not a job for you.

So, there you have it. **Ten jobs which are perfect for teenagers.** One-size does NOT fit all and you'll need to find something that suits your needs, temperament and which you have the skills to "take on" but they are all suitable for individuals desiring to earn an income, work around their own schedules while maintaining their grades.

I've provided you the tips - NOW make it happen. Good luck and happy job hunting.

Additional jobs for teens to consider:

- **Handyman** - If you're good with tools, you can help individuals with a variety of tasks. Minor repairs, plumbing issues, painting and/or repairing fences, etc...
- **Office Help (Receptionist)** - Perfect on a part-time basis to assist with filing, running errands, answering the phones, etc...
- **Youth Coach** - If you enjoy children and are talented in a specific sport, put your talent to work. Work independently with children desiring to improve their skills or with an entire team. YMCA & YWCA are the perfect place to start.
- **Health Spas/Gym** - Often time's gyms will hire teens to clean up the equipment after a day's use.

CHAPTER ELEVEN

WHAT BEGINS WITH THE LETTER "K"?

Kids in the Kitchen

To some parents, the very thought of "kids in the kitchen" may produce images of a disaster in the making, while to others it may remind them of the HUGE smiles upon their children's faces as they added this ingredient and stirred that ingredient into a bowl.

Cooking with kids can be a great experience for the adventurous minded mom, dad, grandparent, teacher or caregiver. It can be done in the kitchen, on the Bar-B-Q grill or over a campfire. And believe it or not, it can be done in the classroom too.

Encouraging children at an early age to help cook supervised meals is one of the smartest and most rewarding things a parent can do for their child. It immediately strengthens the parent/child relationship because the child feels that you trust him/her enough to "invite" him/her to cook alongside you. Teaching a child to cook provides him/her lifelong skills that will prove beneficial as he/she matures and is required to prepare a meal for themselves or meals for others. And it doesn't stop there. So many academic skills are learned or reinforced while in the kitchen. For example, a child will learn about measuring solids and liquids for recipes, weighing items at the grocery store, skills in quantity and quality, estimation, temperature, and telling time. All of these are reinforced while kids are in the kitchen.

Kids in the kitchen shouldn't be taken literally as children can learn to cook just about anywhere. They can cook over a fire pit or campfire when camping, or a Bar-B-Q grill. They can learn to prepare one-dish meals in a crock pot or Dutch oven, a toaster oven or an electric skillet. They might even learn on a hotplate in their dorm room, but let's hope not and prepare them ahead of time.

When growing up, my father was the primary cook in our home. He loved to cook and he cooked extremely well. He'd learned how to cook from his mother who was undoubtedly one of the best cooks on the planet (just ask my college friends, they'll attest to this fact). Although I never received any instruction on cooking, I was expected to prepare certain items for our dinner every night - I can still make a "mean salad" to this day. As a result, I was often in the kitchen when my dad was cooking and I observed everything he did when preparing dinner. But, this did NOT make me a great cook. In fact, I undercooked my first turkey, overcooked the OUTSIDE of the fried chicken leaving the inside raw on my first, second and third attempts, and I failed to include one of the ingredients in my first pumpkin pie which resulted in the foulest tasting pie I've ever eaten.

I decided to teach myself AND my students the first year that I taught elementary school in South Florida. I was hired to teach kindergarten, my dream job. Within the community in which I lived was an Indian reservation. Consequently I had the opportunity and pleasure of teaching several Native American children which blended perfectly with my plan(s) to teach them how to cook. I focused my cooking lesson around our Thanksgiving Feast and when I say feast, I mean F-E-A-S-T. In preparation, my students and I invited guest speakers from the local Indian reservation to share stories about the traditions in their culture. We discussed traditions as experienced by the other children in my class which included many different ethnic groups. My students and I then implemented Steps 1 through 4 of Cooking with Kids below. We took it a step further and invited several members of the Indian Tribe to join us in preparing our Thanksgiving meal. My students and I, along with the female elders from the tribe that participated, cooked sweet potato soufflé, squash casserole, Indian flatbread, corn chowder, creek swamp cabbage, mashed potatoes, green beans, fresh homemade applesauce with blueberries, and Roasted Turkey with orange sauce. For dessert we prepared pumpkin and apple pies. And guess what? THE KIDS SLICED, DICED, MASHED, PEELED, AND CRACKED every ingredient we used, and put together under constant supervision, every recipe we'd selected for our meal. This experience was one of the most memorable and rewarding in my life. Not only did the elders assist us in preparing and cooking our meal, which by the way we did in crock pots, electric skillets, toaster ovens, and using the schools stove/oven(s), but the male elders performed a Native American Thanksgiving & blessing dance in full authentic Native American wardrobe & paints. We enjoyed the most magnificent "authentic" plus traditional Thanksgiving feast and experience imaginable.

Kids in the kitchen should realistically begin with lifestyle and eating habits as experienced within one's family. It shouldn't begin with pouring ingredients into the bowl or placing the burgers onto the grill. It should be an all-encompassing life experience to allow the child to learn life skills. And, who better to teach them than a parent.

Step One:

First, you should assess whether your child is developmentally capable and ready to assist in the kitchen. An example for determining if your child is ready would be if he/she has the physical dexterity and capability required to stir, pour, and hold kitchen utensils without dropping them. It might include when he/she is old enough to understand or have an idea of the types of foods you prepare for your family on a regular basis. Why? Because the first step in Cooking with Kids is planning a menu. For example, if you are vegetarians, you wouldn't want your child to innocently add "steak" or "pork chops" to the weekly menu simply because he thinks it sounds good or because he saw it advertised on a commercial (unless you are willing to cook it and eat it).

Step Two:

The second step in Cooking with Kids is creating a grocery shopping list that you will use when you and your child go to the store to purchase the supplies you will need to prepare the meals. Now, this can be done every day, every three days or a week at a time. And, if you are serious about involving your children then their age should be a factor in how often you shop. A young child will lose interest quickly if you're shopping for an entire week's worth of food, while an older child may have conflicts with multiple trips to the grocery store over the course of a week due to football, cheerleading or band practice. Plan accordingly.

Step Three:

Step three in Cooking with Kids would be teaching your child where items should be stored upon return home from the store. Believe it or not, this is very important. A young child may not realize that ice cream belongs in the freezer instead of the refrigerator. He may think fresh strawberries belong in the pantry, and milk with the juice boxes on the pantry floor. Remember, they are learning and it is crucial that you not only "show" your child where the items belong but explain "why" they belong where you're instructing them to put them.

Step Four:

Step four in Cooking with Kids is to prepare a meal together. If you use recipes when cooking, you will want to have the cookbook opened to the page you're preparing, recipe cards or laptop set up so that your child will see from what source the recipe is coming. If you "create" your own dishes, explain this to your child and perhaps allow him/her to "create" a recipe as well. There is nothing more fun than being creative in the kitchen. Trial and error is part of the learning experience. If you should allow your child to "design" his/her own recipe and prepare the food item, offer suggestions so that the cooking experience and outcome isn't disastrous. This could discourage future attempts at being creative and/or cooking with you.

Step Five:

Step five in Cooking with Kids is serving the meal to the family. This is more than just placing the prepared foods on plates. It should include teaching your child how to set a table with napkins, utensils, plates and glassware. Blessing the food is something that is encouraged in our home. Now, it's time to present the meal to the family and either serve or allow each family member to serve themselves.

Step Six:

Step six in Cooking with Kids is clean-up. It would be nice if upon completion of the meal the dishes and kitchen would clean themselves, but since it isn't likely to occur, teaching this skill in imperative. Many families will differ in this regard. For example, in my home, after finishing our meal and asking to be excused from the table, each individual removes his/her dishes from the table. If food items remain on their plate, the individual scrapes it into the garbage or compost can and rinses their dishes and the sink. Teach your children what is customary in your home. At this point, the dishes are either hand-washed or placed in the dishwasher depending upon the item. Again, this is a lesson worth teaching.

If you're using your fine china that you inherited from your great grandmother, you'd probably prefer that it be hand washed. You will want to instruct your child on which dishes are fragile thus requiring hand washing and which can be placed in the dishwasher. Customarily there will be something left over from the meal.

Perhaps there were more beans prepared than eaten. Teaching your child how to properly store food so that it can be served at another meal, like putting away groceries, is important. Nobody likes spoiled black-eyed peas so make sure that you explain food spoilage to your child. The final step in the cleaning up process is wiping off the table, stove top and counter-tops using whatever method you use. Additionally, cleaning the sink with soap and water is always a good idea.

Outside of the basic Kids in the Kitchen lessons in cooking will be cooking experiences for older children. For instance, for the child who will soon be on his own, perhaps attending college or maybe simply moving out of the family home and responsible for his/her own meals. My youngest son is a perfect example of this need for additional cooking skills. When a child is older, he'll likely want to cook on a grill or use kitchen appliances that will take a little skill to operate. Teaching older children how to use kitchen appliances such as 1) crockpot; 2) rice cooker; 3) pressure cooker; 4) microwave (if your children have never experienced one before); or 5) Bar-B-Q Grill (both gas and charcoal).

These appliances are quick and easy for preparing meals for the on-the-go student as long as they know how to use them and what meals are prepared best in them. It is important that your child have a hands-on experience with each so they feel confident in using these tools. The same is true of using an outdoor grill. Teaching a child how to safely use a charcoal grill so as not to ignite something other than the charcoal and how to ensure that the chemical substances often found in charcoal won't taint their food is critical. Just as critical as using charcoal to cook over is using propane or natural gas grills. Children need to know the safety issues involved with the use of either and parents should teach them. Lastly, teaching children how to use a cookbook or some other source for recipes and most importantly, when cooking meats, the internal temperatures necessary to keep the child healthy and safe from illness or disease.

Cooking with Kids can be a memorable, life altering experience. It promotes a bond between child and parent that will last a lifetime. It teaches children life skills essential to their development into young adult and throughout their adult lives. It is fun experiences that can and should be shared will all members of the family. And, the greatest benefits of  all.......are you ready for this one? Children who cook for themselves and others will eat what they've prepared 9 times out of 10. Let me repeat that. If they cook it.....they will eat it. So parents, let's get cooking!!!

If for some reason you find that you are unable to "cook" with your kids, there are resources available to assist in teaching your children how to cook. Just visit this website to find out how.

http://www.youtube.com/watch?v=dTtVMxgH-eU.

CHAPTER TWELVE

WHAT BEGINS WITH THE LETTER "L"?

Children are Products of their Environment and Learn what they Live

Leading by example is what every individual on earth should make an effort to do for the sake of others for it is the examples that we set that lead to the roles our children (and others) see us live.

The world famous poem, *Children Learn What They Live*, by Dorothy Law Nolte is the perfect "blueprint" for parents, caregivers and even teachers in terms of how they should live their lives in order to put forth the best example for those that rely upon and look up to them as role models. It is a phenomenal tool for reminding parents and adults alike how we should treat one another as it provides an excellent point of reference allowing adults to restore themselves and regain their perspective when dealing with children, their spouses, significant others, co-workers and anyone else with whom they engage on a personal and professional level. Suffice it to say that the poem is a reflection of the inner wisdom that every human-being should embrace.

The first verse of the poem, "If children live with criticism, they learn to condemn" is very powerful. First of all, as I've expressed many times before, children are like sponges. They watch, learn and repeat most of what they see us do. Even when we don't think they are watching or listening to us, more than likely they are. They'll repeat what they hear us say; emulate our tone of voice when communicating and even mimic our gestures and body postures. This verse says a great deal and means so very much. For instance, if our children observe us being critical of others, or perhaps we're critical of our own children when they've not completed a task to the best of their ability, or perhaps the world in which we live, we're teaching them to condemn, not only others but perhaps themselves. Instead of teaching them about the good in others and the world around us, we're teaching them about everything that is wrong.

Children, and some adults, are sensitive creatures. A simple glance, odd tone of voice or even gesture can imply dissatisfaction even when nothing of the sort is intended. The way that we say things can hurt others, so it is important to "think BEFORE we speak." Sometimes we say things before we actually think the words through. Perhaps we are frustrated by something that occurred earlier that day or perhaps you're in a hurry and you say and/or respond to someone without realizing that your preoccupation with something completely unrelated has made its way into your statement or tone of voice. You hear the same words, and tone, that the recipient hears as it leaves your mouth. Wow! The damage is done......or is it? Absolutely not, but only if a parent takes the necessary steps immediately following the incident to correct the situation with their child. By recognizing the impression that you've just made, you'll want to apologize for your tone and/or words. This simple act alone will help to prevent this "Mole hill" from becoming a mountain. It will also eliminate the minor mishap from damaging the child's sense of self-worth which is the ultimate goal when situations such as this occur.

The way that we say things to others, and the tone and words that we use, should be carefully considered whenever we are frustrated, angry, disappointed, upset, afraid and even hurt. Words are very powerful and can injure others in very profound ways. The perfect example that I'm sure you'll recognize is when a parent or teacher uses criticism as a tool to encourage children to do better. Unfortunately, children (nor adults) respond well when criticized. They often interpret it as a personal attack which ultimately will be received like a trip to the doctor to receive a shot or an increase in taxation.

Similarly, nagging, which is completely ineffective in soliciting change in behavior should be eliminated from your bag of tricks. Nagging, which is a form of complaining, doesn't inspire but instead "brings down" individuals. It focuses more on deficiencies, disappointments and difficulties and not on solutions. An example which demonstrates the power of words and the way in which they are delivered to encourage the same end result might be: "Sam, it's time to join the group for circle time - find a spot on the carpet" vs. "Sam, we'd love for you to come join circle time with us and there's a perfect spot right beside your friend Matthew." Of these two directives, the second will more than likely elicit the desired response and Sam will feel good about joining the group.

To truly bring about change in ourselves and those that we love and care about, being positive is the manner that proves beneficial and productive will often encourage the

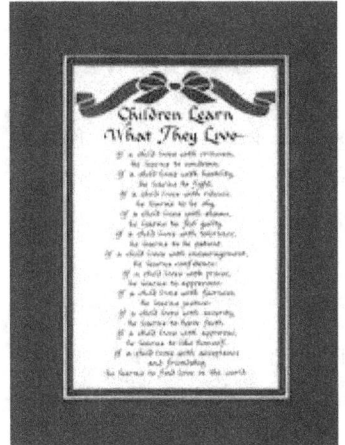

desired behaviors in others and will often improve one's self worth and esteem. By eliminating "negative" tendencies that we may have used in the past or perhaps are still implementing when dealing with others, we should instead encourage and model positive and creative solutions that are going to inspire instead of discourage those around us.

Remember, words are very powerful. They can be used to inspire others and their thinking or discourage them equally. Inspiring others through the use of kindness, support and encouragement will prove more beneficial to everyone and will inspire and motivate positive transactions and self-esteem. When individuals are made to feel good about themselves and their accomplishments and to recognize their potential, they'll respond in the manner which will enable them to "reach the stars".

From the inspirational poem, *Children Learn What They Live* by Dorothy Law Nolte, we can find many valuable life lessons. Lessons that will help us learn from our feelings, actions and reactions, and how to teach others how to recognize, manage, and learn from their own.

In the second verse of the poem, "If children live with hostility, they learn to fight", the overall point is to help every one of us recognize our feelings and then how to successfully manage and deal with them without the need for hostility or losing control in a situation.

With violence being so prevalent on television, movies, and video games and even within our world, children have had incredible exposure(s) to hostility and fighting. Living within an environment full of hostility, many children become vulnerable. Unfortunately, some of the children who live in hostile environments may begin to develop a "tough guy" image always ready to "jump into" trouble when they come upon it or even seeking it while other children may become incredibly frightened as a result of hostile environments leaving them unable to handle conflict within their lives and/or environment. Neither of these developing personalities is appropriate and/or what we'd desire for our children. So, how do we ensure that our children are not hurt in any way through this exposure?

Monkey See-Monkey Do; Better Described as Children See Then Do What We Do:

As explained in verse one of the poem, children are like sponges that watch and learn from others. On the forefront, are their parents who will often model behaviors that children will learn most of life's lessons from directly and even indirectly? How parents resolve differences and handle different familial crises, either through destructive hostility or by using constructive dialogue and resolution, will often dictate how children learn to deal with conflict. Choosing the most constructive manner in which we resolve conflict will prepare our children how to do so too.

Every member of a family has conflict within their life, whether it is the result of feeling left out on the playground, getting a poor grade on a test or being passed over for the much anticipated promotion at work. Therefore it stands to reason that on any given day, each member of a family will come together at some point during with burdens that they've carried with them along the way. One little trigger can send one, if not everyone, into a heated environment, even if the "conflicts" aren't related to anyone present. Learning how to "put out the fire" instead of fanning the flame is the key to properly managing such conflicts.

Focusing on constructive methods in which "each" member of the family can address their feelings of frustration, even if in silence, is paramount to reducing the likelihood that these feelings do not escalate out of control. Teaching and modeling acceptable methods of releasing tension may be necessary, especially for younger children who may engage in throwing, hitting and/or biting others.

Teaching Positive Conflict Resolution:

For younger children, it is always constructive to teach them acceptable methods of releasing energy - perhaps running around the yard, painting a picture or role-playing with dolls, cars or parents. Older "tweens" may feel ridiculous exercising the once accepted methods of distinguishing tension and may need other solutions such as listening to and/or dancing along to their favorite music, playing an instrument or washing the dog or perhaps the family vehicle. Adults, too, need to learn appropriate ways of handling the day's frustrations especially when in the presence of others. Perhaps taking a deep breath (or four), going on a brisk walk or even "taking a time out" to regroup if necessary. Whatever the choices, as long as they provide the much needed release without being destructive and/or inappropriate, should be encouraged and implemented when necessary.

In the perfect world, we'd all be capable of NOT losing our cool and shouting and/or insulting others when we're feeling overwhelmed. Unfortunately, this isn't a perfect world which suggests that from time to time each of us will behave inappropriately and say and/or do things that we shouldn't have said and/or done. What now? How we handle ourselves after we've "lost our cool" is just as important as learning "how to" handle ourselves before the situation gets out of control.

An Unfortunate Scenario:

For instance, while walking out of the house on his way to school, a child accidentally breaks a vase when the book-bag draped over his shoulder knocks it off the table as he turns around in the hallway to say "goodbye". This event is a perfectly innocent scenario that unfortunately results in a broken vase, huge mess to clean up and panic on the part of the child. In reality, this situation will more than likely result in the teenager being yelled at by his mother for being careless and perhaps horse-playing when in fact nothing of the sort had occurred. It's human nature to assume things that simply don't apply, or perhaps didn't occur and react accordingly. In this situation, an accident truly did occur and the response was harsh and probably hurtful. After all, the child was being considerate and offering a "goodbye" before rushing off to school. What now?

Learning how to handle "situations" or pick up the pieces immediately thereafter is necessary in order to reduce the tension, hurt feelings and demonstrate more appropriate ways of dealing with situations when they occur. In the example above, the mother should have stopped and gathered herself and her thoughts BEFORE responding to the sound of the crashing vase. Unfortunately, the situation escalated and now diffusing it is necessary. By providing both an apology and an explanation in this particular instance, the child will feel better about him and the situation and will more than likely be able to enjoy the rest of his day without the overwhelming guilt, frustration and anxiety that would surely have followed him had his mother not apologized for her hurtful words.

Learning to express oneself verbally, and honestly, is something that everyone needs to know how to do. This does not mean ranting and raving resulting in more harm than good. It does mean, learning to communicate in a constructive manner using dialogue that will allow others to understand your feelings and frustration(s).

Anger is NOT our Enemy - How We Choose to Handle It Can Be:

Children, and adults, need to learn that everyone gets mad from time to time and that there will invariably be disagreements between members of the family. Learning how to express anger appropriately, handle conflict and resolve disagreements is the key to how it is interpreted by others and how they are left feeling when all is said and done. Often, following arguments and/or disagreements, children will be left feeling confused and unsettled.

By providing an explanation to children that there was a conflict that needed to be resolved and that neither mom nor dad was sure of the best way to handle the matter and this made them upset and frustrated, you will help children understand that even though there was a problem, mom and dad are working together to solve it. It is also imperative at this point that parents apologize to their children about how their words, tone of voice and actions may have made them feel frightened and uncomfortable and assure them that next time they will try another problem-solving strategy that will prove more beneficial to everyone.

It is through this and other life lessons, that a child will understand that everyone loses their temper and must learn how to control it in better ways. It will provide the foundation necessary when teaching children how to handle conflict and resolve problems in creative and appropriate ways vs. hostile and frightening ones. Teaching and understanding that anger is normal and something that we all feel and should learn to express appropriately is part of growing up and living with other people. It is through teaching, modeling and implementing different strategies that our children will develop their own strategies which will ultimately determine the pattern(s) that they will take with them into their adult lives and implement into the lives of their children and families regarding conflict resolution.

CHAPTER THIRTEEN

WHAT BEGINS WITH THE LETTER "M"?

Teaching Children Manners

Children offer their parents and other adults less respect than in the "good old days" when we were young. When I'm out and about and witness children cussing at or in front of their parents, observe them rolling their eyes and speaking in a tone of voice that would make "Mother Teresa" cringe, it makes my skin crawl.

This is not to say that ALL children behave in this manner. In fact, thankfully I see many well-behaved, courteous and mannerly children in my daily adventures which make me take a deep sigh of relief. Having the opportunity to "see for myself" how these parents engage and interact with their children is quite pleasing and provides hope that perhaps one day, the majority of the children will be alright.

Like anything in child development, children must be taught manners and how to behave politely. By beginning at an early age they'll establish better relationships with children and adults throughout their lifetime. By the age of two, children are quite capable of responding to modeling good behavior, polite manners and other details associated with manners. Therefore, parents must remember that children will emulate what they see for themselves. For instance, a child that hears obscenities day in and day out will more than likely develop the same form of language patterns him/herself. So be cautious, children are little sponges. They absorb everything that they are exposed too.

Manners "START" Here:

Teaching Toddler's Manners

It is important that beginning when children are at or around the age of two is critical to teaching him/her good manners and polite behaviors. At this time, the interaction between child and adult is at an all-time high. We are assisting them in learning and expanding their vocabulary, fine & gross motor skills, but more importantly skills associated with communicating with others.

At this point, we are teaching toddlers the "polite" way to communicate his/her needs. It is through repetition and modeling that we encourage our children to use polite words and actions to secure the things that they desire. For instance, teaching a toddler to use the word "please" is paramount to the manner in which the child's requests are received by others. As children, adolescents, teenagers and adults, this doesn't change. The manner in which an individual goes about communicating with others will often dictate the response they receive.

Top "4" "Magic Words" to Teach your Toddler: Words to Last a Lifetime

1. ***"Please"*** is a word that often results in a positive response. It is received by others well and tends to provide the outcome desired (when within reason). For instance, a toddler who says, "May I please have a cookie" will more than likely receive the cookie (if the time is right). A teenager asking for a brand new sports car for his 16th birthday, lathered with "Please" may not have the desired result. But, it was sure nice to hear the word used in a sentence.

2. ***"Thank You"*** is something that should automatically follow phrases using the word "please". In fact, teaching one without the other is quite pointless. Individuals of all ages like to hear the phrase "thank you" after a deed is performed or a request has been honored. This doesn't go away with age. In fact, it often means a lot more the older the individual still exercising good manners.

3. ***"Excuse Me"*** is another vital phrase that children should be taught....especially when we're on the phone!!! It seems that children ALWAYS need our attention when we are engaged in a conversation with others, personally or over the phone. Teaching a child these two simple words allows them to "interrupt" in a polite manner indicating that they need our assistance or attention at that time. It certainly beats the other option which is the child repetitively calling out one's name, tugging on your arm or throwing a loud temper tantrum. These two simple words can be taught to be used at other times too such as when a child burps aloud, bumps into another individual or other various bodily functions.

4. ***"I'm Sorry"*** is one that suggests that a child understands his/her actions and can be used to make the individual "hurt" or "saddened" feel better. As most of us

know, this phrase will be used throughout our lifetime and one that should be included in your list of polite behaviors & manners as without it one will suffer immeasurable when he/she cannot establish or maintain interpersonal relationships with others.

Although teaching manners may require a child reaching a certain age, using them indefinitely should follow-suit. For without manners, people will often find it difficult to be accepted by others, or perhaps shunned for a lack of manners and basic interpersonal skills.

Children's Relations with Adults:

Teaching children the "basics" isn't enough. As parents, grandparents or simply adult-figures to children, we all need to encourage children to use acceptable manners and behaviors. Without encouragement, and modeling, we cannot expect children to continue using them. Simply because we've taught them to ask for items using the word "please" doesn't mean that he/she will remember to do so each time. That is when we need to step in and remind them of the correct and polite way to ask for things. Telling a child once isn't good enough. It is something that we'll have to do over and over again until the behavior becomes second nature. (It's like teaching a husband to put the toilet seat down!!! How many times must we take a dive screaming in the middle of the night BEFORE he learns)? Perhaps we should put the lid down so that he splashes himself when he visits the bathroom in the middle of the dark night! (I'm just kidding because we'd then have to clean up the mess).

Top "10" Manners Beyond the Spoken Word:

In addition to teaching children a "polite" vocabulary, teaching children how to interact and engage with others is necessary. For instance, teaching a child how to address someone upon meeting for the first time is a wonderful lifelong skill. I've been so pleased and proud to observe as my two sons extend their hand to "shake" hands upon meeting someone new and introducing themselves. Good manners don't stop here. Let's review a few additional "good manners" that every child (and adult) should learn and practice.

1. **Standing Up** - this is critical to exercising good manners when a "lady" walks into the room. Women can do it too, especially if the lady entering is elderly. Teaching

young boys this polite behavior certainly shows that he is respectful of the individual entering the room.

2. **Shaking Hands** - extending a hand to "shake" those of other individuals that they are meeting for the first time or to show respect at times thereafter is an excellent interpersonal skill for not just men but women too - especially in the business/corporate world. It is actually a universal gesture of goodwill.

3. **Smile** - a smile can break the ice better than just about anything else (unless you've watched the commercials where a Coke is offered). Many individuals feel uncomfortable when approached or expected to engage with individuals wearing a frown. A smile typically encourages others to "feel at ease" thereby opening the door for interaction. This is true for both children and adults.

4. **Eye Contact** - establishing eye contact is an important manner to teach children. By teaching a child how to make eye contact he/she will be able to show a level of respect to the individual with whom they are addressing.

5. **Mr, Mrs, Miss or Ms** - these words should be encouraged of your children when engaging in conversation with adults. It is a sign of respect and one that most adults in a position of authority will expect when being spoken to. It is a gesture of respect.

6. **Removal of Hats** - most of us raised in the South understand that when you enter a building, sit down to a meal, or salute the flag, removing a hat is customary and a sign of "good manners" and respect. Teaching children this is important and will certainly assist them as they enter school.

7. **Dining Etiquette** - this area is one that I could spend hours on but will just focus on a few specific details. Since when did it become appropriate to bring games, toys, or even talk or text on the cell phone while at the dining table. Beyond that, what about elbows on the table, standing in one's seat, or placing feet on the table? And probably most curious is the overwhelming number of people that carry on conversations with their mouths full will spew food across the table. It seems today "anything goes". And this isn't just at home, but in school lunchrooms and restaurants too. I know many families are busy these days with crazy, hectic schedules making it difficult to sit down and enjoy a family meal, but seriously, making "table manners & etiquette" a top priority no matter where you're eating will go a long way in your child's inclusion in activities around mealtime.

8. **Tissue Please!!!** You probably know where this is heading, but in the unlikely event that you do not, please teach your children about "picking" their nose using a tissue and disposing of it properly. Enough said!

9. **Profanity** - for whatever reason some children think that the use of profanity is "cool" or makes them more "adult-like". If you're using this type of language at home around your children, there is a good chance that your child will use it too. Sadly, using profanity tends to "severe" relationships among certain peer groups. In fact, even relatives will tend to discourage and/or even prevent outings with others that overuse profanity. Talking like a sailor is offensive to many unless perhaps you're a pirate out at sea. However, if you're not, you might want to clean up your vocabulary and teach your child how to do so too. More offenses at school result from foul mouthed children and recently I've learned of "teachers" using this type of language too. It suggests that you have absolutely NO manners and even less respect for the individual(s) with whom you are conversing or within the presence of. Profanity goes hand-in-hand with saying unflattering, insulting things about others too. Be careful how you discuss business associates, or individuals that you have a "beef" with in the presence of your children. You'd be surprised at how many details they'll remember, share with others and use to suit their own situations.

10. **Telephone Etiquette** - equally as important as the others mentioned but on a serious level. If you've decided to allow your children to answer the telephone, teaching them the proper way to do so is imperative to individuals leaving messages or calling back again. Sure, if it's a solicitor you may be just fine with a rude child on the answering end. However, suppose it's your pastor, employer, best friend, mother, father, or Aunt Gertrude. Children shouldn't be answering the telephone and assigned the task of taking messages if they've not been properly instructed on how to do so. For example, teaching a child (if you're not present) what to inform the caller is mandatory to rule-out foul play. Should you be present but unavailable, a child should know who to take a proper telephone message so that you will be able to return the call at a more convenient time. You never know when it could be an emergency and the individual needs to make contact with an adult or competent child. It's THAT important.

A child who has been taught good manners and to behave politely will be well served as he/she matures, grows and begins interacting with others. Teaching children the necessary and perhaps, socially acceptable, manners and ways to behave is something that parents, teachers, and caregivers should take seriously and devote whatever time it takes to ensure that the child is prepared. Not only will these manners serve you in your interactions with the child well, but it will allow the child to develop stronger interpersonal relationships with others.

Philosophy of Montessori Education

There are varying philosophies supporting different educational practices used within school systems throughout the United States and abroad. Each is based upon the various models of study, Plato and Aristotle being amongst the earliest theorists to develop said philosophies. Over the years, parents, students and educators have continued to explore the different philosophies and how each impacts learning and while each philosophy has its own belief behind it as a driving force, none has been proven to be more effective than another. In fact, when comparing philosophies one will find many differences and similarities amongst them.

There are five basic philosophies of education:

- *Perennialism* - A very conservative and inflexible philosophy based on the view that reality comes from fundamental fixed truths, especially as they pertain to God. It believes that people find truth through reasoning and revelation and that goodness is found in rational thinking.
- *Idealism* - Believes in refined wisdom. It is based on the view that reality is a world within a person's mind. It is based upon the belief that truth is in the consistency of ideas and that goodness is an ideal state to strive to attain. In practice, individuals believe that schools exist to sharpen the mind its intellectual processes and students are taught the wisdom of past heroes.
- *Realism* - Based upon the view that reality is what we observe - the world as it is. It believes that truth is what we sense and observe and that goodness is found in the order of the laws of nature. In education, schools exist to reveal the order of the world and universe. This philosophy stresses teaching student's factual information.
- *Experimentalism* - The foundation is based upon the belief that things are constantly changing. Based heavily upon the view that reality is what you experience. Truth is what works right now and that goodness comes from group

decisions. Schools therefore exist to discover and expand the society within which we live and provide social experiences and problem solving application.

- ***Existentialism*** - This philosophy believes in personal interpretation of the world and is based upon the view that individuals define reality, truth and goodness. Education exists to aid children in learning about themselves, specifically "who" they are and their place in society. Subjects are discussed freely within the classroom environment.

From each of these philosophies, educators have developed learning strategies that are modeled within classrooms in part based upon a healthy combination of each of the philosophies above.

While the names have changed to better suit educators, one such philosophy that is widely practiced today is more commonly known as Montessori Education. As I discovered while talking with parents throughout the years about the philosophy that I used in my classroom, which was combination of Montessori and the Dewey philosophy "learn by doing" with a heavy emphasis on science and critical thinking, it was quite clear that many were unfamiliar with the underlying basics of many educational philosophies including Montessori education and most couldn't conceive that children, left on their own to explore, would do nothing more than play. I also learned that when put a different way, most parents did understand that a great deal of learning comes from play and exploration.

"Montessori", put simply, is a developmentally appropriate approach to learning which allows success across all social strata and includes learning opportunities for children with special   needs.

What is Montessori Education:

One of the most widely known philosophies on education, developed by Maria Montessori, an Italian physician, educator and philosopher, is based on several key factors most importantly that children are natural learners and that by providing a "child sized" environment for learning through implementation of self-guided and self-corrected education, children will thrive while learning.

Key Concepts of Montessori Learning:

- Through Montessori learning, we are able to foster competent, responsible, adaptive citizens who are lifelong learners and problem solvers.
- Learning occurs in an inquiring, cooperative, nurturing atmosphere. Students increase their knowledge through self-initiated and teacher-directed experiences.
- Students learn through the manipulation of materials and while interacting with others. These experiences are both meaningful and are precursors to the abstract understanding of ideas and concepts. Learning is gained through the use of one's senses. (See my article on
- Students are considered as a "whole". Learning focuses on physical, emotional, social, aesthetic, spiritual and cognitive needs and interests of each child and is considered inseparable and equally important.
- A strong emphasis is placed upon the respect and caring attitudes one has for oneself, for others, our environment and all life.

Montessori teachers are educated in multiple areas including:

- Human growth and development.
- Classroom leadership skills that will provide for a nurturing environment that is both physically and psychologically supportive of learning.
- Exceptional observational skills which allow the teacher to provide activities and materials that match students' developmental needs allowing the teacher to guide her students in creating their individual learning plans.
- Teaching strategies that both support and facilitates the unique and total growth of each individual.
- Research capabilities which provides unlimited resources for learning materials and activities that can be used to design developmentally responsive, culturally relevant learning environments in which all students will thrive.

Montessori classrooms will include the following basic characteristics at all levels:

All Montessori exercises employ movement, manipulatives, free choice (within limits) and a point of completion. They are usually self-correcting and help develop the child's sense of order, concentration and independence. The Montessori methods in teaching Practical Life,

Sensory, Language, Mathematics, Science, Geography, History, Art and Music cultivates the child's adaptation and ability to express and think with clarity.

- A classroom atmosphere that will support social interaction, encourage cooperative learning, peer teaching while strengthening emotional development.
- Teachers who are educated in the Montessori philosophy and its methods of education and proficient in the implementation of its practices at the age level they are teaching and capable of insuring the key concepts are put into practice.
- Heavy emphasis on partnering with the family as it is an integral part of the individual learner's total development.
- Children will be heterogeneous in nature and will include children of different ages and grade levels.
- Materials will be available to provide for the diversities within each class including the provision for activities and experiences fostering physical, intellectual, creative and social independence.
- A classroom schedule which provides for large blocks of uninterrupted time for discovery, exploration and problem solving allowing for the interdisciplinary connections of knowledge while allowing for the creation of new ideas.

As you can see, Montessori education focuses on the "total" child and encompasses a large variety of learning tools and strategies in order to provide a "whole" learning experience. Many of the "Montessori" practices have been implemented within the public school classroom(s) including multi-grade classrooms which encourage peer teaching, cooperative learning opportunities, "center time" which allows for self-discovery and uninterrupted time in which to do so, as well as providing an atmosphere for "hands-on" learning and for social interaction.

Let's focus on some of the more critical elements of Montessori education:

1) Multi-Age Grouping:

Rather than group the children by age as is typical in the public and private school sector(s), Montessori places them in a mixed-age class. This type of classroom arrangement mirrors a real community, while teaching tolerance and respect for others.

By incorporating a mixed-age approach, older students are encouraged to become role models, mentors and leaders to the younger students. Research strongly supports that mixed age grouping offers children opportunities to teach each other and develop leadership skills. This provides a wonderful way to build confidence and solidify what the child has already learned.

The 3-year age span, which is commonplace for Montessori classrooms, allows a child to remain with the same teacher for the duration of that time period. This allows the teacher and child to bond while allowing her to understand the child's learning style and how best to foster his/her love of learning.

2) Smaller Classroom Size:

A low teacher-student ratio means that the students are afforded many opportunities for one-on-one learning. It also allows for teaching to take place in smaller groups without the distractions often found in classrooms with larger numbers. The teacher is able to monitor the students more closely and personally than is possible in high teacher-student ratio classrooms allowing a close bond to be formed between the teacher and her students, adding to each child's sense of self-confidence and security.

3) Teacher as a Guide (Guided Learning):

Teachers in Montessori classrooms have a less conspicuous role than does the traditional teacher. Instead of sitting at a desk in the front of the room directing students who are crowded into a designated space often in rows of desks, teaching the same concept to every child at the same time, the Montessori teacher is able to circulate among the children, teaching them individually or in small groups. Children work on mats on the floor or at tables and are actively involved in their education as opposed to passively listening, often bored and not in-tune with the instruction taking place. Each student is given the opportunity to pursue his or her own interests, under the teacher's guidance while engaged in meaningful learning activities. After being given a lesson on a particular subject, the child is free to return to that material at any time and practice it until he/she has mastered the concept. It is the teacher's job to assess when mastery is achieved, and then give provide the child his/her next lesson. Detailed record-keeping on each child is critical to this process, as is observation.

4) "Hands-On" Approach to Learning:

Hands-on and experiential learning approach is core to the Montessori philosophy. Hands-on teaching materials provide the child learning experiences that they can grasp at an early age. Later, they are able to understand these at an abstract level. For example, four-year-olds are introduced to four-digit numbers with hands-on materials which they can manipulate. By the age of five, they are adding these numbers and are introduced to the other operations of subtraction, multiplication and division. All of this makes sense to the child and is not intimidating but exciting.

Hands-on learning materials isolate each step of learning. Rather than overwhelming the child with a great deal of new information all at once in an abstract manner, children are able to use these materials while learning step by step in a concrete way. They work with each piece of equipment until they reach a level of mastery.

5) Self-Paced Learning Environment:

Again, just one of the many philosophies of education, Montessori has served its students and their families well in providing a learning environment which allows for children to learn at their own pace while providing for other critical elements in the developmental process. This may be one of the greatest differences between Montessori and traditional education. By allowing children to "learn" at one's own pace, they are neither held back nor pushed ahead beyond their capabilities. They are self-paced and self-motivated to do the best they can personally, but without the pressure of competition and comparison.

6) Learning for the Sake of Learning vs Being Taught to Test:

The primary and sole reason or emphasis of Montessori education is on the process of learning, not the product of a completed worksheet or test. Knowledge comes from the children asking questions, not being given the answers. Montessori students are encouraged to study things of interest for themselves and make their own discoveries during the process. The curriculum covered is the equivalent or superior to what is taught in traditional schools as it actually expands upon the basics, AND it is not geared to provide an end result such as a higher standardized test score. In fact, children in Montessori classrooms are not taught to memorize and regurgitate facts, but rather to understand them as they relate to a greater whole. Montessori curriculum is a collection of integrated studies providing a holistic educational experience. It is designed to engage a child's whole mind while sparking his or her imagination.

7) *The Importance of Self-Discipline:*

Self-discipline is necessary for genuine learning and growth. Montessori discipline is a child's ability to control him or herself from within, which stems from the child making correct choices. Montessori education provides a multitude of opportunities for making choices and decision making each day. Teachers encourage their students to assess the effects of their choices, both on themselves and on others. Peace education and conflict resolution are taught and practiced in Montessori schools. Children with differences of opinion discuss their source of conflict at a "peace table". When a conflict is resolved, the children announce "We declare peace" and return to their activities. Peace education is taught in a variety of ways enabling them to see how it will be applicable in their lives as they mature and grow.

8) *The Freedom to Move:*

Children in Montessori classrooms are encouraged and able to move about freely to converse with other students about their lessons. This is important for the development of social skills as well as providing them opportunities to help one another academically. Research shows that children perform better when they can move around instead of being expected to remain seated for long periods of time. Children love to work collaboratively at all levels, although most notably in the elementary grades.

9) *Individualized Education Plans:*

A term used in public schools when discussing specific tools and resources that will be utilized in "adjusting" a child's curriculum to better suit his/her individual learning needs. In Montessori classrooms, each student enjoys the benefits of an individualized education plan that would be hard to achieve in a traditional classroom setting. Montessori teachers track each student's individual progress and teach according to the child's pace and learning style. Only the cultural subjects are taught as a group, but even then the children are free to pursue activities or research of their choosing after the combined lesson is complete. Both math and language are taught based upon the academic levels of each student, while providing a comfortable level of challenge to the child.

Although some may question the philosophy of "self-discovery, problem-solving and uninterrupted blocks of time" in which to do so, one cannot dispute the fact that many children who've attended Montessori schools have grown up to be very successful adults. Many accomplished scholars have enjoyed to benefits of Montessori education including Larry Page and Sergey Brin, both Co-Founder(s) of Google; Jeffrey Bezos, Founder of Amazon.com; Katherine Graham, Owner/Editor of the Washington Post; Jacqueline Bouvier Kennedy Onassis, Editor & Former First Lady; Anne Frank, Author of The Diary of Anne Frank; Prince William and Prince Harry, English Royal Family; Julia Child, Chef, Star of many TV Cooking Shows and Author; Gabriel Garcia Marquez, Nobel Prize Winner for Literature; Peter Drucker, Management Guru; T. Berry Brazelton, Pediatrician and Author; Sean 'P. Diddy' (Formerly Puffy) Combs, RAP mega-star to name just a few.

If you're considering Montessori learning as an alternative to traditional public or private school education, I encourage you to schedule an appointment and visit a local facility. You'll be amazed and I'm quite certain pleased with the learning environment and the level of self-disciplined, happy learners.

CHAPTER FOURTEEN

WHAT BEGINS WITH THE LETTER "N"?

Welcoming a New Baby Home!

The addition of a new member to the family is always a time of much anticipation, great excitement and even some level(s) of anxiety shared by many. Parents are typically elated and are usually prepared for the arrival of the new bundle of joy as they've had nearly ten months to plan and prepare. However, for others, such as the "once upon a time" only child it isn't always that simple.

For many children, the addition of a new family member is quite frightening. They've spent month's watch their parents plan, prepare, share their "exciting" news with others and basically redirect a great deal of their focus and attention on the impending arrival. To those children, the new sibling is often regarded as a threat. Someone who has taken away the attention once directed only toward them. It is a time when, with younger children, a lot of developmental regression may take place. For instance, a child that was nearly potty trained may require diapers all over again. Or the child's sudden need to have a security blanket, stuffed animal, pacifier or some other "comfort" item with him/her at all times. The child may even suddenly have difficulty going to sleep at night or desire to sleep in bed with mom and dad.

What can you do to make the transition less emotionally stressful for the existing children?

Here are a few suggestions:

- **Spend quality time daily with the child or children that you already have at home**. They need to know that they are still JUST as important, lovable, interesting, exciting and deserving of your time and attention as they were BEFORE you found out you were expecting another child. And don't wait until the new baby arrives to begin. Your child will need to strengthen his/her bond before the baby arrives. This will comfort them and eliminate unnecessary stresses that they might be feeling.

- **Allow your children to get accustomed to the fact that there will be a new child** but don't make every conversation with your children about the arrival. For instance, "aren't you excited about having a new baby brother or sister?" becomes annoying for young and old children alike. When you're speaking to your other children, talk about things that are of interest to them specifically including their interests, hobbies, and favorite this or that.....make the conversation(s) ALL about them.
- **Teach the "new" older sibling how to carefully coexist and handle a new sibling**. This is especially important if the children will be close in age. I've heard about many new babies coming into the families of students that I've taught who haven't been welcomed especially kindly or handled carefully. In fact, one child actually took a "popcorn" popper - push toy and attempted to clobber the new baby with it. It is imperative that children know how delicate infants truly are and how to touch, handle and care for them. Practicing with "lifelike" infant dolls is a good method for teaching siblings the proper techniques for handling an infant, rocking, assisting with diaper changes, feeding, etc....Children are going to want to participate so it is better to ensure that they know what is appropriate and not appropriate by allowing them "hands-on" opportunities with an appropriate sized replica.
- **Mommy-Time**. Remember that once the baby arrives there will be many changes within the home. Mom will naturally be spending a great deal of time with the new baby especially if nursing. But, the older sibling(s) will also demand mom's attention. Dads, grandparents, aunts and uncles will all need to step in and help mom with the infant so that she'll still be able to devote undivided attention to the other children. No matter what, moms aren't easily replaced. Grandmas are nice but moms will always take the cake. Dads are super but they're no replacement for mom's lap, special kisses or hugs.

Slowly, but surely, your children will learn to accept their new sibling. It isn't easy going from "top dog" to "wait your turn, mom's busy feeding your new brother". You'll need to exercise a great deal of patience and compassion. Sometimes allowing the older siblings to approach at their own pace is necessary instead of the immediate inclusion in the baby's activities. For others, you may actually have to prod them a little bit so they aren't simply a spectator.

Depending upon the atmosphere at home, your child will more than likely differ from another family when welcoming a new baby home. In other words, "one size doesn't fit all". You'll want to consider the temperament, age differences, family dynamics such as blended family, etc....when bringing home a new child.

Don't forget about family pets. They also feel the strain when a new family arrives home. You'll want to include them when introducing the newest family member. It's just like introducing a new pet into the home. Before your furry friend was your primary focus. Now it has to share your affection with a tiny person which may be stressful for the family pet. When my daughter-in-law brought her new son home from the hospital, her dog did not handle being banned from the bedroom and family bed. He had to be prescribed pills for depression after several weeks of chewing his hair off, shaking and various other odd behaviors which started immediately upon the infant's return home. Over time he adjusted and was given the same freedoms as before, but for a while there he was quite a mess.

If you're reading this because you've just welcomed a new baby into your family, Congratulations and good luck.

CHAPTER FIFTEEN

WHAT BEGINS WITH THE LETTER "O"?

Childhood Obesity - A New Epidemic

There is an unsettling epidemic of childhood obesity in the United States and various countries throughout the world. Childhood obesity has tripled in the past 30 years. Obesity in children is a serious medical condition that affects children of all ages. In fact, the prevalence of obesity in children and adolescents aged 2 to 19 years of age is about 17% (2008) a slight decrease from the previous calculations of 19.6% in the 1980's and affects about 12.7 million children. Between 2011 – 2012, 8.4% of children ages 2- to 5-years of age were obese compared with the 17.7% of 6- to 11-year olds and 20.5% of 12-19-year-olds were obese. The number of obese children is staggering and puts these children at a higher risk of developing obesity-related disorders such as diabetes, heart disease, high blood pressure and high cholesterol. Additionally, children who are overweight are often known to suffer with low self-esteem and from depression.

Definition of Childhood Obesity:

The definition of childhood obesity is simply a child that is well above the normal weight for his or her age and height.

Symptoms:

Parents should not confuse a child carrying extra pounds as a child that is overweight or obese. In fact, some children will have larger body frames than that of the average child meaning that their bones are going to provide additional weight. Children will also carry increased amounts of body fat during certain stages of development. If you are concerned about your child's weight, a doctor can calculate your child's BMI (body mass index) which will determine whether your child is overweight or not. During this evaluation the doctor will determine your child's percentile based upon comparisons with other children his or her age and of the same sex. These figures are often calculated and referred to as "percentile" such as in the example: "Your child is in the 80th percentile" which simply means that your child, when compared to other children of the same age and sex, is larger than 80% of children compared to.

Causes:

Obesity is the result of a caloric imbalance which means not enough calories are being used in relation to the number consumed although it can also be linked to genetic, behavioral, hormonal and environmental factors as well. It is typically the result of children eating "too much" and exercising "too little" to burn the calories consumed. It is unusual for genetic disorders or diseases to be the culprit although two have been identified, Prader-Will syndrome and Cushing's syndrome however they affect a very small amount of children.

Physical inactivity has been attributed as a major contributor to childhood obesity in that it has been noted that over the past 20 years, children have been ever-increasingly "glued" to visual media such as computers, television, and video games whereas two decades ago children were more inclined to enjoy physical activities like touch football, chase, basketball, tennis and/or any other form of recreation where physical mobility was required and enjoyed. Unless children make a conscientious effort, physical activity is something that children will go an entire day without. In fact, another contributing factor is the phasing out of physical education programs within our schools. Instead of children receiving daily physical education classes, they're lucky to receive those three days per week and even less in the middle and high school years.

Physical education in our school systems should not be held entirely responsible for obesity in youth. It is a parent's responsibility in large part to teach children how to eat properly in terms of quantity and the foods they consume. Parents should model behaviors that encourage their children to get physical and exercise in some capacity whether riding a bicycle, going for a brisk walk, swimming, playing sports or doing anything age appropriate to get the blood flowing through their child's veins.

Risk Factors:

Usually, there is a combination of factors that result in a child becoming overweight.

Diet: Wide access and the inclusion of high-caloric foods in our diets is a major contributor. Eating fast foods due to hectic schedules preventing mom from cooking, an overwhelming desire for baked goods and snacks from vending machines can result in children (and adults) putting on extra pounds while ultimately lead to obesity if the child is immobile for most of the day. Soft drinks, candy and other beverages high in sugar, fat and calories are also a tremendous problem for adding extra pounds.

Lack of exercise: Physical activity seems to be a thing of the past unless you consider children's fingers since they seem to get more activity than every other muscle in their bodies. If children don't engage in physical activities, they won't burn calories. Without burning calories, they'll gain weight. It's that simple.

Family History: Although this isn't always the case, children who are members of families who are overweight tend to emulate poor eating and exercise habits thereby becoming overweight themselves.

Psychological Factors: Sadly, with the fast paced society in which we find ourselves, more and more members of our society, including children, are soothing themselves with food. Children will overeat to cope with emotional problems and in lieu of dealing with problems that they face. Often, overeating can be linked to stress levels or even to boredom. Latch-key children may eat more than children involved in after-school activities.

Family Habits: If your pantry is filled with high calorie food items such as cookies, chips or if you tend to visit the drive-thru often, your children will more than likely be overweight even if they are physically active. By eliminating your child's access to these types of caloric foods, you may prevent your child from gaining excessive weight.

Socioeconomic Factors: Studies have indicated that children from low-economic backgrounds are more likely to become overweight. Sadly, it takes both money (resources) and time to prioritize exercise and good eating habits.

Complications Resulting from Obesity:

There are many forms of complications that can result from obesity including not just physical, but social and emotional elements as well.

Physical Complications: Most notably is the potential for the child developing Type 2 Diabetes. This is a chronic condition that affects the way a child's body metabolizes sugar (glucose). It is often attributed to poor eating habits (diet) and a lack of exercise. Often the results can be reversed or at least reduced by exercising regularly and eating a nutritious, healthy diet.

Metabolic Syndrome: This syndrome refers to a group of conditions that can put a child at risk for the development of heart disease, diabetes or other health problems including high blood pressure, high cholesterol and excessive abdominal fat which is linked to the aforementioned heart disease.

High Cholesterol & High Blood Pressure: Even though you may not believe it, a child can develop either of the two health issues above especially if he/she practices a poor diet. Each complication contributes to the development of plaque within the arteries causing the arteries to narrow and harden leading to the possibility of a heart attack or stroke.

Asthma and other Breathing Difficulties: With an increase in weight, children may find it difficult to develop a healthy set of lungs which can result in asthma or other related problems.

Sleep Disorders: Children who have developed breathing difficulties due to childhood obesity may experience sleep apnea which is a condition that will result in your child snoring or developing abnormal breathing when he or she sleeps. This can be a very serious condition so you'll want to monitor your child's breathing when he/she is sleeping.

Early Puberty or Menstruation: Obesity can lead to early development and hormonal imbalances. These imbalances can result in early onset of puberty.

Social & Emotional Complications:

Even though one might not consider these complications as serious as the previous, physical complications, this type can lead to very serious consequences for a child.

Low self-esteem and bullying: Children can be cruel especially when an overweight or obese child is present. Being teased and bullied by others leads to reduced levels of self-esteem and an increased risk of depression.

Behavioral and/or Learning Problems: Due to increased levels of anxiety than their normal or average sized peers, overweight children have difficulties in social situations due to poor social skills. Some overweight children may begin to misbehave or "act out" in an effort to disrupt their classrooms. Others may become socially withdrawn avoiding contact with others thereby failing to establish social connections to their peers. Higher levels of stress and anxiety may also interfere with learning as extreme levels of worry may lead to academic failures.

Depression: Often when children suffer from low self-esteem they can easily develop feelings of hopelessness. When a child feels as though there is no hope for improvement in their life, they begin to experience feelings of despair and depression. Children who suffer from depression will lose interest in many things, require more sleep and may often cry for no apparent reason. Some depressed children will be able to hide their feelings or suppress them to others which can have extremely devastating outcomes should these feelings remain undiscovered.

Treatment and Prevention of Childhood Obesity:

Healthy lifestyle habits including eating healthy and participating in daily physical activities can lower the risk of become obese and developing related diseases. When encouraging healthy lifestyle habits, it isn't enough to encourage your children while you, the parents, continue to practice and live by another set of standards. Healthy lifestyles should be practiced by everyone within your home. Modeling proper, healthy eating habits and requiring that your children do the same will be much easier if the "unhealthy" food items high in sugar, fats and calories aren't a part of your pantry's contents. Equally, exercising must be encouraged and should be practiced by all members of the family. Exercising together whether it is bike riding, going for walks around the neighborhood, playing volleyball or basketball for 30 minutes at a time can be an excellent tool for losing excess weight and preventing it. Additionally, by engaging in physical activities together, you'll be able to spend quality time as a family doing something that will benefit every one of you – including the family pet.

Obesity doesn't have to get the best of you or anyone for that matter. By planning a healthy menu at the beginning of the week, including a shopping list that you will not deviate from, you'll be able to ensure that you and your children are eating healthy without the possibility of slipping into or falling back into the poor eating habits that lead to the place that you find your child. Additionally, just like planning a menu, you should plan physical activities that everyone can participate and keep a schedule to ensure that you do engage daily. A child should participate in physical activities no less than 30 minutes per day to remain physically fit and 45 minutes if they suffer from obesity or from being overweight.

For more information on living a healthy lifestyle and learning how to modify your current habits, visit this link, Get the Real "Skinny" on Healthy Weight Loss – Commit to a Lifestyle Modification and Get Results and learn how you can truly make a difference in your lives.

CHAPTER SIXTEEN

WHAT BEGINS WITH THE LETTER "P"?

Living with Peer Pressure

What is Peer Pressure?

Have you ever found yourself in a situation where you were being encouraged to do something that you felt really uncomfortable doing? Did you agree to go along with the individual or group or did you hold true to yourself and your values and refuse? If you gave into the pressure(s) being placed upon you by others, you became a victim of negative peer pressure. If you were able to deny the insistence, suggestion or pressure by others, Congratulations!

Sometimes, and for many reasons, we find it difficult to say "no" to others. Why? If I had to guess, I'd probably say for a multitude of reasons. Perhaps you were afraid that you'd hurt someone's feelings or maybe you were worried that you'd be looked upon differently by others. Perhaps you REALLY wanted to participate and the least bit of encouragement from your peers was all it took to sway your decision.

What you are experiencing in situation(s) such as this is **Peer Pressure** and there are two types: *Positive and Negative.* Most of us are aware of, either from word of mouth, reading or personal experience, Negative Peer Pressure which is being asked, encouraged or told to do something that you typically would be opposed to doing. Peer pressure, in teens, is fueled by a teenagers need to feel accepted, approved of, and belonging to certain social circles. Sadly, due to one's desire to feel a part of a group, good judgment can be impaired resulting in participation in risk-taking behavior(s) and dangerous activities. Often peer pressure is responsible for driving a wedge in between a teen and his/her family resulting in the positive influences of the family being reduced or eliminated. Usually, negative peer pressure leads to feelings of deep regret within the teen and can result in very negative outcomes. An example of negative peer pressure would be a teenager that is encouraged to throw a pool party when his/her parents are away on business even though he knows the "house rules" forbid this activity. Although his/her friends are enjoying the party, the teenager has gone against what he/she knows is correct and right and feels a sense of remorse and/or the fear of being caught by his/her parents. Peer pressure is a force to be reckoned with. If you don't think so, remember Jiminy Cricket. (Let your conscience be your guide).

On the other hand, there is also Positive Peer Pressure which typically presents itself as a form of encouragement or suggestion to do something desirable that perhaps wouldn't have otherwise been done without the suggestion having been proposed and/or presented. Positive peer pressure can result in a teen's energy being "super charged" and is often reflected through his/her new motivation for success. Positive peer pressure may include a new desire to emulate a classmate's study habits to improve grades in an effort to be "college" material. It might be the sudden urge to join a tennis team or chess club because someone that you admire is participating and enjoying another aspect of teenage life. Positive peer pressure is normally associated with more desirable outcomes and appropriate behaviors.

Why Do Children, Teens & Adults Fall Victim to Peer Pressure?

Peer groups for young children, teenagers and adults are a normal, necessary and healthy part of an individual's development. It allows us, as individuals, to develop our identity, and provides us with a "support group" for discussing problems, sharing information, improving our social skills and exploring our values. Within this group, we are able to interact with those whom we consider our equals thereby promoting our independence. By spreading our wings and building new relationships, *we are able to develop our sense of self-worth and our level of self-confidence.* Sometimes, even within our social arena, we can fall victim to negative forms of peer pressure.

Being unable to resist the temptation(s) of negative peer pressure can be a result of many things more often than not it is due to one lacking self-esteem or self-confidence. It can be attributed to wanting to "fit in" or belong to a certain social group enough that we are willing to throw our good judgment out the window just to be a part of the desired group. This is common of individuals who don't necessarily have a peer group or group of friends with whom they can engage socially. You might even feel that "if you do this" whatever **THIS** is, you'll become more popular or get noticed by a cute girl or boy that you've had your eye on. Problem is, although you may get noticed or even become popular for a day or even a week, your popularity may not be the type you were hoping for and in fact may result in the formation of negative opinions about you by your peers.

Dealing with Insecurities & Building Self-Esteem:

We all suffer from insecurities from time to time whether it is not feeling good in the outfit that we've chosen to wear to our best friend's party, because we feel overweight, or as a result of missing the field goal that would have won the Homecoming Game. It's normal and it's a part of life. Insecurities go a lot deeper and can severely impact their very existence.

Throughout our daily lives, experiences that we have contribute to our level(s) of self-esteem and self-confidence. These experiences also contribute to our feelings of self-worth. As early as our primary school years, our esteem is being impacted although we are far too young to realize it is happening. Perhaps you were the lucky little girl that all the other girls (and boys) admired and invited to their birthday parties and sleepovers (boys not included). These childhood experiences undoubtedly boosted your level of confidence helping you "blossom" into the popular teenager. Maybe you're the athletic boy who was good at everything from mathematics to baseball and everything in between. Whatever the set of circumstances, it appeared that ALL the other boys (and girls) wanted to hang around you on the playground, in the lunchroom or on the bus ride or walk home. Unbeknownst to you, these allegiances affected your level of self-esteem and self-confidence.

On the contrary, but with very much the same impact on levels of self-esteem and confidence is the child that got head-lice and everyone found out about it shunning him/her and labeling him/her "cootie kid". Or, it could have been something as insignificant as wearing an older brother's hand-me-downs which resulted in being poked fun at by your peers. Kids are cruel - no matter what parents and adults want to believe and because of experiences such as these or similar in nature, some children develop lower levels of self-esteem and lack confidence in themselves.

Our confidence and self-esteem will be affected for as long as we live **IF** we let it. Being able to recognize how even the most ridiculous little things, or even "HUGE" things as we perceive them to be, can wreck our self-image is paramount to rising above the influences and peer pressure of others.

A child's level of self-esteem and confidence is hugely influenced by his/her parents and family. Parent who have established and maintained an open and loving relationship with their children raise teenagers that feel proud of their unique talents and traits, are confident as a result of their accomplishments and capable of establishing their self-identity. Typically these children are able to learn from their mistakes and / or failures without a reduction to their level of self-confidence. Because they are secure in their family relationships, they often feel more secure in forming relations with others without any significant presence of insecurity.

By ***establishing relationships with peers who share the same or similar interests***, adolescents and teens will be able to develop a personal identity resulting in less dependence on their parents. We've all heard the saying, "choose your friends wisely." There is a good reason for this saying and it is extremely important that you exercise good judgment when doing so. Selecting a peer group should be about choosing individuals with whom you admire and can be yourself. It should surround you with people who share the same or similar values and moral character. This group will provide you teen companionship, emotional support and provide a sense of belonging that you desire outside of your family. Choosing a group of people with whom you admire but with whom you have very little in common can lead to increased feelings of insecurity which can ultimately result in your doing things to "fit in" that typically you would not do and shouldn't have to do.

Peer relationships can last a lifetime although some may not last more than a particular school year as people and things change. Our personalities change, our interests change and so will those of your peers. If you and a peer go separate ways, it is probably for a very good reason. Don't let it destroy "who" you are, "who" you've become, or "who" you will be. The time that you spent within the relationship provided you both life experiences, an opportunity to develop social skills, establish relationships with others and grow.

Knowing who you are and how important you are can be difficult especially if you've been the victim of cruelty and bullying from your peers or within a particular social environment. As easy as it is to say, it's a difficult thing to overcome you must be able to put the nonsense behind you and rise above the influence. You are what you imagine yourself to be. Don't fall victim to the self-fulfilling prophecy unless your prophecy is to be a great person and do great things!

When I was in high school, I had a classmate who wasn't very popular due to his hobbies and interests. They weren't considered mainstream by many of the athletes or more popular students. Although he participated in sports, he wasn't one of the "jocks" as they were called. He was kind, considerate and made an effort to befriend everyone as truly this is one of the most effective ways to "*win friends and influence people*" thereby reducing the level of criticism and mocking that he received on a daily basis. I enjoyed his company and his friendship and because we were friends I was privy to his innermost feelings of rejection and humiliation by classmates. He was a classic example of an individual who, at the hands and tongues of others, could have given up and allowed the immaturity and inability to exercise good judgment of others to destroy him. Instead, fifteen years later when I returned to my high school for a class reunion, he was the "*highlight*" and "*success story*" of the evening. While the jocks, for the most part, were bald, overweight and out of shape, he was muscular, tan and "A NEW MAN!" He'd risen above the influences of criticism and cruelty and re-established himself in the image that he'd created for himself. He utilized his hobbies and interests to become a very successful professional photographer. I was so impressed and proud of his achievements and so were those who'd ridiculed and insulted him so many years before.

Believing in yourself is something you must do no matter what others may say or feel about you. Never allow anyone to get the upper hand. If you feel confident you'll exude confidence. If you believe you're equal to your peers, nothing should make you feel less. This is not always an easy thing to do. By surrounding yourself with the correct peer group, you can do anything you set your mind too as you'll have a built-in support system. But just in case you need a little boost in this area, there is a book that I will recommend to you that will provide you the necessary tools and skills to re-establish yourself, build your confidence and improve your level of self-esteem entitled, ***How to Win Friends & Influence People***, by Dale Carnegie. This book has been helping people for many years and is just as helpful today as it was when it was first published over seventy years ago.

Avoiding Peer Pressure Victimization:

We all want to be popular or at least have an opportunity to socialize within popular groups of our peers. Sometimes at the risk of our health and well-being, we choose to do things that we believe will enhance our popularity that we wouldn't otherwise do. Negative peer pressure is like being bullied. You are bullied into doing things that you ordinarily wouldn't even consider and normally at your *own* expense. Knowing how to "defend" oneself against peer pressure is similar to standing up to a bully. Every person needs to know how to effectively handle the pressures put upon us by our peers whether it is a classmate, boyfriend, girlfriend, co-worker or acquaintance. How do you prepare to "face-off" against peer pressure? Here are a few suggestions:

Five Step Plan to Handling Peer Pressure:

1. Having a clear idea about where you stand on key issues such as sex, drug use, drinking and smoking is the first step to overcoming negative peer pressure. If you are firm in your beliefs on each topic, you will be in a better position to stand your ground without deviating outside your pre-determined limits. **NEVER** be afraid to speak up and let others know your boundaries. You may catch some "grief" if your attitude and stance on the topic isn't the most popular, so be prepared. For just as many jaunts as you'll receive, you're likely to receive an equal amount of respect.

2. Like role playing "how" or "what" you might do if you are bullied, this tactic may prove beneficial in handling certain situations in which you are being pressured to engage. Practice and rehearse what your response might be should someone pressure you on the above topics and others so that you aren't caught off guard.

3. Avoid bullying others. Making other people feel bad in an effort to "fit in" is wrong on all levels and can lead to some pretty harmful consequences. If you are pressured to engage in activities that may cause harm or fear to another person, you should never participate. By stating clearly your objection, you may motivate others to follow your lead.

4. Be a leader and set a good example for your peers or others with whom you associate. By establishing yourself as a leader amongst your peers, you will naturally be in a position to influence the decisions and actions of others. Use this leadership role to your advantage in reducing the frequency of negative peer pressure and the negative consequences that typically result.

5. Exude confidence and comfort with your decisions and choices. If you display a hint of hesitation or wavering in your stance against peer pressure or being pressured, you will provide the "other side" with the fuel in which to prey upon your weakness. Instead of getting caught up in the moment when peer pressure is taking place, remember that your choice to engage in or refuse will be something you must live with. Focus on how you feel about what is occurring and then express your opinion. Do not allow yourself to be intimidated.

Peer pressure can come in many different forms from bullying to bribing and from many different fronts. Whether it is your best friend or your boyfriend, knowing how to avoid being pressured is imperative. Being confident of whom you are and what you believe is right and wrong, acceptable and unacceptable will provide you the very foundation that you need to avoid being pressured into things that you aren't comfortable doing. Knowing who you are and having established limits based upon moral character and values that you hold dear will provide you the means to ward off the pressures. Sometimes the simplest way is to firmly say, "NO" and remove oneself from the situation or group presenting the pressure. The word "NO", which we all learned as a toddler means "not to any degree or manner; not at all; refusal, denial or disagreement...in all languages. Avoiding negative peer pressure can be that simple.

Peer pressure works ONLY if you let it! Be assertive and stand your ground. If you refuse to let others intimidate you, peer pressure loses its power.

This article is dedicated to the students at Whitewater High School and Whitewater Middle School located in Fayetteville, Georgia. Please rise above the influence.

Attached is a special message from DiGiTiLsOuL. Please take a moment to watch the attached video and share with you pre-teens and teens:

http://www.youtube.com/watch?v=nan-xiVUOAo&feature=player_embedded#

Are you Poisoning Your Children & Family?

Every day, unbeknownst to most consumers, we are using products that are unsafe, toxic potentially deadly. Even with all of the information that is made available online and in print, many consumers are simply unaware of the dangers that we're exposing our children, pets and families to on a daily basis. You or someone you know brushes their teeth, washes their hair, cleans their home, applies lotion(s) to their bodies, and even washes their clothes daily but what you might *NOT* know is that you and they are unknowingly applying and/or using products that have been known to be associated with many childhood and adult-onset illnesses.

Consumable products contain harmful toxins and ingredients that have been linked to allergies, birth defects, psychological abnormalities, skin reactions such as eczema, headaches, depression, joint pain, chronic fatigue, chest pains, dizziness, loss of sleep (insomnia),cancer, diabetes, ADHD, Asthma and reproductive illnesses plus many other health-related disorders. Ingredients such as bleach, which is a registered pesticide with the Environmental Protection Agency; ammonia; and formaldehyde (known to most consumers as an embalming fluid and represented under nearly 40 different trade names on the labels of many consumable items) is used as a cheap preservative in numerous household products. We use many products topically or around our homes while some we ingest, virtually inviting these chemicals into our bloodstream.

How do you know which products to avoid? As I've said before, knowledge is power. By researching and reading labels on the products that you and your family use, you can eliminate many of the toxic products in your home. Read the newspaper, watch the news (I know it is terribly boring, full of commercials and LOTS of depressing information) - BUT, you need to do what you can in order to know the facts.

There are many toxins in our daily lives, it's hard to know where to start. I'm going to provide you with a place to start by sharing a few products that you more than likely are using in your home, around or upon your family.

Top "5" Products that Have Been Linked to Health-Related Disorders & Illnesses:

The first on my list is sure to make you cringe...especially if you're a new mom (or a mom of many years).

1. ***Johnson & Johnson Baby Shampoo or Wal-Mart's label Equate Tearless Baby Wash.*** A *class action lawsuit* which was filed a few years ago, accuses Johnson & Johnson and Wal-Mart Stores of selling shampoo and baby wash that allegedly contains_**methylene chloride**, an ingredient banned by the FDA in cosmetics because it's linked to cancer. The law firm that filed the lawsuit is also investigating ***Target's Night-time Bath and Body Wash,*** which is not currently named in the suit. If you or someone that you know is currently using either of these products, read the label and spread the word. You might have to do a little digging as like formaldehyde, harmful toxins are known by multiple names. Do your homework and make certain that you and your loved ones are safe.

2. ***Conventional Laundry Detergents.*** Most people are unaware that conventional laundry detergents contain a host of *toxic and carcinogenic chemicals* that are detrimental to our health and our ecosystem. The ingredients contained within can be divided into many categories of ingredients including: surfactants (chemically derived from oil) that reduce surface tension in water enabling the removal of dirt from fabrics. Problem is that typical synthetic surfactants like **diethanolamines** that are slow to biodegrade and become carcinogenic upon entrance into the atmosphere.

Another category of synthetic chemicals is optical brighteners which make clothes appear whiter as they convert UV light wavelengths to visible light. The problem with brighteners like **aminotriazine** is that it is not biodegradable and according to the Environmental Protection Agency, 2010, cause bacterial mutations in aquatic environments. It's important for consumers to remember, as many don't even think about the fact that the skin is the largest organ in the body and is responsible for both elimination of and absorption. By wearing clothes that have been laundered in toxins that make-up many laundry detergents, the toxic chemicals are exposed and absorbed into the skin through skin cells thereby providing more chemical exposure to the human body resulting in damage to the person wearing the clothes and to the local water sources as well.

3. ***Toothpastes.*** Recent studies have shown that there are some dangerous chemicals in toothpastes as well. One such chemical, **triclosan**, was included in toothpastes as it was believed to help remove tartar and clean teeth better. Studies have revealed that the chemical has been identified to upset the balance of an individual's endocrine system and can result in the generation of bacteria strong enough to resist antibiotics. This chemical is so prevalent in consumable products that the chemical is being found in urine samples in as many as three quarters of the United States population.

4. ***Cosmetics and Body Products.*** Buyer(s) Beware!!! The cosmetic industry is one of the largest and most profitable industries in the nation. In fact, both consumers and health care providers need to be aware that there are literally thousands of *toxic synthetic chemicals* used in cosmetics and personal care products such as soaps, body washes, and deodorants that do not include a complete disclosure of ingredients on the labels. Men, women, and young girls of means have been exposed to unusually high levels of the toxic chemical **lead** used in many consumable personal care products. Because cosmetics and personal care products are used more heavily than most consumable items, wouldn't it make sense to avoid using products **containing a lethal combination of toxic and carcinogenic ingredients**? Cosmetics and many other products including foaming cleansers, body mists & lotions, lipsticks, skin creams, moisturizers, shower gels & body washes, antiperspirant and deodorant, lip glosses and hand lotions contain **synthetic chemical preservatives known as parabens**. This ingredient is readily absorbed through skin entering the bloodstream. It has been known to exert estrogenic activity on breast cells and has been linked to the development of malignant tumors. Often manufacturers hide this toxic ingredient under *fragrance* which can then be masked by a term that covers over 2,000 different chemicals including carcinogens and other equally harmful toxins.

5. ***Household Cleaning Agents.*** Many families use toxic cleaning products in their homes every day without even realizing the dangers. Many of the cleaning agents that we use actually contain many harmful chemicals. Common household products such as sanitizing sprays and wipes, garden pesticides, paints, batteries, detergents and flea powders are not only hazardous to humans but to the environment as well. The toxic chemicals contained within each product affect our

environment by contaminating our groundwater, lakes and oceans. If ingested, absorbed through the skin or inhaled, they can result in illnesses that may not appear until many years later. Many *common household cleaning products are actually classified as hazardous waste* and should not be disposed of in the trash but instead at a hazardous waste collection center. Besides the pollution to our environment, our health and the safety of our children are at risk. Chemical levels inside the home can be over 70 times higher than levels found outside. Each year, thousands of household poisonings are reported - many fatal. Of those reported, approximately 70% occur in children between the ages of one and five years old and are a result of improper or unsafe storage of  dangerous cleaning products and medications. Many adults do not understand the significance of toxic substances brought into the home. For example, dishwashing detergent holds the record for the greatest number of accidental poisonings. Dandruff shampoo, if ingested, results in the degeneration of vital organs; household ammonia when mixed or used in combination with bleach is a **DEADLY** substance; and bug spray/insecticides can remain active and airborne in a home for up to 30 years. Yikes!!!! The *most common and dangerous ingredients* in household cleaning products include **alkalis** which are soluble salts that are effective in removing dirt without a lot of scrubbing and can result in burns and internal injuries or death; acids which are great for removing hard-water deposits, discoloration and rust stains but irritate and can cause injury to skin and eyes. Oxalic acid, most commonly used in toilet bowl cleaners is very poisonous.

There you have it - a list of everyday consumable products that consumers should be wary about purchasing and using around, in and/or upon their homes, pets and loved ones.

Just because the items can be purchased in your local department or retail store does not mean that they've been tried, tested and deemed safe. In fact, this couldn't be farther from the truth.

Although many chemicals found within our homes are used for vanity, health & hygienic reasons and to make our lives easier, we really don't consider the long-lasting and sometimes immediate ramifications and/or consequences of using many of these substances. Be careful - cautious - and consider using alternative non-toxic products that are economically and ecologically more sensible and which will not expose you and your loved ones to toxic chemicals that ultimately may alter their lives in a negative manner.

Go Green!!!

For more information on safe, consumable products and/or to learn about safer products for you and your family, please visit www.randaleeroberts.com and complete the "Contact Me" page or visit my website at www.wahunation.com watch the short video and then click on the *More Information* tab. It is private and your information will NOT be shared with anyone. Or, you may contact livingearthfriendly@gmail.com with your question, contact information; the best time to reach you (including your time zone if you don't want a call in the middle of the night) and I'll get back to you as quickly as possible).

Promiscuity in Teenage Girls

A few years ago when picking up my oldest son from his high school I noticed a young girl getting into the car ahead of me. As she bent over to place her things into the backseat, the rather short skirt that she was wearing lifted so far in the back that is was clearly noticeable that she was wearing NO underwear - no briefs, panties or even a thong. I nearly got out of my car and approached the vehicle to make her mother aware of her daughter's wardrobe malfunction. I imagine that if I saw what I shouldn't have, many others did too!

After watching the car drive away, I wondered if the attention that she gained from wearing no underwear was the "type" of attention that she was hoping to gain or if in her rush to get ready that morning she'd simply forgotten to put any on - it could happen I suppose.

The next week at a volleyball game I began inquiring with several male and female students at the high school as to the attention-seeking behaviors that girls (and boys) used in an effort to gain the attention of the opposite sex. I was both shocked and alarmed.

There are many psychological reasons for female promiscuity but the most common reason noted is related to a lack of attention by a girl's dad (male parent) either due to divorce, death, neglect or just indifference. The level of promiscuity increases if the male parent departs when the girl is young, especially prior to the age of 5 years. Often these girls will look for a male "suitor" to fulfill their *Electra complex*. What is an Electra complex? It is the unconscious tendency of a daughter to be attached to her father and hostile toward her mother. Sadly as these young ladies pursue a male, the males will engage the girls in the game of seduction which can ultimately result in the female being in over her head and perhaps participating in activities that she might otherwise have avoided until a more appropriate age and time. Additionally, once the seduction game has begun it is often very difficult for the girl to stop.

Promiscuity has also been used by many females in an attempt to "hurt" the men they loved and that left, whether it a dad, boyfriend or husband. Through promiscuity, some females feel that they are regaining power. It is very similar to the "jealousy" game often played using sexuality to hurt someone who previously hurt them. This cycle can be vicious. Sadly, when girls find someone that isn't a *runner* they'll do anything and everything both consciously and subconsciously in an effort to determine his allegiance and to determine if he'll be there for the long run. Some girls are afraid about a repeat offense only this time with the man she's chosen to love. This type of scenario may actually destroy a positive relationship resulting in the girl being left again.

With the exposure that children have to sexually explicit materials these days including television programming, commercials, movies, the internet and music lyrics, it's no wonder anyone is capable of leading a normal age-appropriate life. In fact, statistics have revealed that with the assistance of mass-market media encouragement children are taught that "sex appeal" is a personal quality and one that they need to develop to its fullest. We're unintentionally putting our children at risk when we allow exposure too many forms of media. Most families don't want to remove the television, radios and computers from their homes so perhaps monitoring the selections and setting "locks & limits" will minimize some of the content regularly marketed to younger children, pre-teens and teenagers. A short review of some of the statistics uncovered revealed the following:

- 83% of the top 20 shows on television contained some sexual content including 20% with sexual intercourse.
- 42% of the songs on CD's contained sexual content; 19% contained direct descriptions of sexual intercourse.

- On average, music videos contain 93 sexual situations per hour including eleven "hard core" scenes depicting intercourse and oral sex.
- Research conducted concluded that girls who watched more than 14 hours of rap music videos per week were more likely to have multiple sexual partners and be diagnosed with a sexually transmitted disease.
- Prior to parental uproar, a very popular clothing store marketed a line of thong underwear decorated with phrases such as "Wink" and "Eye Candy" to 10-year old girls. These types of media influences can be part of the reason our youth are so confused and misguided.

Often and most common is the teenage girl lacking self-confidence and/or self-esteem that practices promiscuity to gain the affection and/or attention of the opposite sex. In high schools there tends to be a great deal of "sexual competition" as well as many opportunities for sexual engagements. In fact, if your teenager doesn't talk to you or share with you about the "on-goings" at school and parties, you might want to inquire with him/her or another parent with whom you've established a relationship as the information that you learn will definitely inspire you to become more involved. You'd be shocked to know what is going on in your area with teens.

While adults have the capacity to recognize and understand that sex is merely a means to an end and in no way, shape or form will it create a binding agent as it relates to love (other than perhaps an unplanned pregnancy which will forever bind a non-couple) teenage girls may not. Sadly, the girl who uses sexual promiscuity to land the fish will eventually run out of bait and the hooked fish will get away. For the girl the same pointless cycle will continue to repeat itself as she attempts to be noticed by the opposite sex with the same outcome. The girl is quite possibly incapable of realizing that this behavior is not working or is futile although she may convince herself that she is beautiful, popular and desired by many.

Another common example of teenage promiscuity is when the teenager sees a guy with whom she finds attraction and begins the chase. She dresses promiscuously and perhaps inappropriately i.e. short skirts, low-cut shirts, tight shorts or jeans leaving nothing to the imagination, no bra or even underwear, clingy clothing, etc... in an effort to attract him sexually. Shortly after meeting, she's jumping in the sack with him and confuses sex with love. Girls who are unable to differentiate true feelings of love from puppy love, sex, infatuation and lust are typically those that will move-in with a young man only to have the relationship (sex) fall apart within 3 to 6 months when they "break-up". This cycle is often repeated.

Parents, it is up to us to break the never ending cycle. Evidence suggests that commitments and values can vary from school to school, county to county (even within a county) and state to state making curriculum difficult to tackle in schools. Research suggests that parents and religious beliefs are a potent one-two combination when it comes to influencing a teenager's decision(s) regarding whether to have sex or practice abstinence. Parents are and should be the most influential person(s) in helping their teens make the decision to abstain. How can this be done? It can be as simple as:

- Maintaining a warm and loving relationship with your children.
- Letting teens know that they are expected to abstain from sex until marriage. (Although it might not happen but if you don't discuss it, they won't know your opinions and the reasons behind them).
- Encourage and maintain an open line of communication with your children. Never avoid or feel uncomfortable (in their presence) about discussing "sensitive" issues with your children (and if you are - put on your game face). If your children feel comfortable talking to you about issues that are serious in nature although often "embarrassing" they won't choose to go somewhere else for the information, i.e. friends, internet. Wouldn't you rather provide sound guidance, counseling and advice to your child over a friend on the football team or cheerleading squad with whom you have no idea what they'll advise?
- When parents are involved in their children's lives and share their religious and moral value system with them, they will see less risky and immoral behavior(s) from their children. Morals are not abstractions. Parents and other adults with whom your child associates must demonstrate good moral decisions and teach them through proper modeling the differences between devotion and infatuation in order for them to process and make the distinction in their hearts and minds.

Teenagers, especially teenage girls, need to be counseled and guided to understand the difference between sexual relationships as a way to fill the void that they are experiencing from either the loss of a male parent or even indifference as demonstrated by their father or as a method of establishing a false sense of self-worth or self-esteem and love. Sex does not equal love and if a child is attempting to obtain the love that she is missing from her father, sex is not the answer. She may give but she'll never receive what it is that she's looking for in return.

Please talk with your teenager today **BEFORE** it is too late and the vicious cycle begins.

For additional information on Teenage Sexuality and Promiscuity, please visit:

http://www.psychiatric-disorders.com/articles/warning-signs/teenage-sex.php
http://www.bmei.org/jbem/volume2/num3/mays_teenage_promiscuity.pdf
http://articles.student.com/health-sexuality/sexual-health/promiscuity-a-teen-age-epidemic

CHAPTER SEVENTEEN

WHAT BEGINS WITH THE LETTER "Q"?

Quitting Is NOT an Option – Persistence Always Pays Off

How easy it would be to just throw up our hands in disgust when things don't work out the way we'd planned. It happens every day when someone tries something and the desired outcome is anything but. Unfortunately, many parents allow their children to "give up" without a fight instead of encouraging them to push on. These same parents are often those that did the same thing when they were young, and perhaps as adults too, since this type of character quality is one that lingers and follows individuals throughout their lifetime. It isn't something to dwell upon in shame or something where we should place blame. This type of attitude and behavior can be modified with a little positive thinking, effort, and reinforcement.

What would the literary world be like if authors threw in the towel every time they received a "no" from a publisher after they attempted to write the next great novel, children's book, or play? After all, every great movie began between the covers of a book. We'd live in a world devoid of entertainment in many forms. What about athletes who weren't successful the first time around. Congressmen and women, singers, musicians, and corporate CEO's have probably all experienced doors being shut in their faces - each having to decide whether to press on or give up. Most chose to be persistent and it paid off such is the case of Bill Gates whose first attempt at business failed when he and the co-founder of Microsoft, Paul Allen, launched Traf-O-Data only to fail; or Walt Disney who failed many times in business only to become one of the most well-known names in family entertainment, not to mention an incredible businessman.

As an author myself, another man who triumphed after many failed attempts was Theodor Seuss Giesel, aka Dr. Seuss, an author that thankfully never gave up. After countless manuscripts were denied, he just kept plugging away until one day he got it right. In fact, it took twenty-seven submissions before he was able to get his first book published - the ever so popular, *The Cat in the Hat*. This tremendous author, known as one of the most distinguished children's book authors of all time, has sold over 222 million copies of his books which have been translated into 15 different languages.

Now just think, *Green Eggs and Ham, One Fish, Two Fish, Red Fish, Blue Fish, Horton Hears a Who!*, and more popular than ever, *How The Grinch Stole Christmas* would have never made it onto the bookshelves, into our homes, or onto the big screen if Dr. Seuss had given up. Instead he was persistent. He pushed ahead even harder working countless hours mastering his skill and using the knowledge obtained from his studies until he was finally published.

In my opinion, Theodor Seuss Giesel paved the way for many authors. He showed all of us that "If at first you don't succeed, try, try again" is a better methodology than washing our hands of the task at hand. This philosophy is one that ALL of us should emulate. It would certainly make each of us better people. Just think what we could accomplish if we enveloped Dr. Seuss' way of thinking, incorporating the same will to succeed into every little thing that we desired to accomplish making our dreams a reality.

I challenge each of you to teach your children about the wonderful Dr. Seuss sharing his trials and tribulations that led him to become the successful author that he was. I encourage everyone to allow their minds to soar to new heights and "do" what it is that they desire to achieve by simply **NOT** giving up. Establish a goal, envision the outcome, and then reach it! It's that simple......and *EVERYONE* can do it.

Thanks Theodor Seuss Giesel for setting the bar high and having the tenacity to achieve your dreams. I dedicate this chapter in your memory on the anniversary of your death, and that of my birth, September 24th. You are a true inspiration to me and to other aspiring authors and achievers.

CHAPTER EIGHTEEN

WHAT BEGINS WITH THE LETTER "R"?

The ABC's of Reading

Teaching a child to read is one of the most rewarding and invaluable lifelong skills you can do for your child, grandchild or student. Reading and language development begins early in a child's life, as early as infancy. Parents that sing to and read aloud to their newborns are planting the seeds that will eventually lead to the joy of reading and/or storytelling by their children.

While compiling research for this article, I discovered many blogs and articles regarding what is considered to be the appropriate age for teaching children to read. Some felt that Kindergarten might be appropriate while others preferred first grade and above. Others felt that teaching them as early as possible was acceptable. My question, why is it necessary to put an age limit or requirement on teaching a child anything intellectual in nature?

In an earlier chapter, *Interacting with Your Newborn*, I addressed the different stages of development up until age one and encouraged specific interactions that stimulate and encourage different forms of learning. I identified the fact that children begin learning at a very early age and can be taught many things without even realizing they are learning from our interactions with them.

Teaching your child to read should be no different. For instance, teaching a baby to use sign language to communicate his/her needs and desires until the child is capable of communicating verbally is one step toward language development, just like singing songs, reading stories and coloring pictures to tell a story, sorting shapes and identifying colors are used to encourage language development and reading skills.

When I began teaching, I had the opportunity to choose my internships of which I had "four" specific semester long opportunities. I elected to teach beginning in a Head Start program and classroom with four year old children, followed by Kindergarten, first and second grades respectively. I did this because I wanted to experience first-hand the developmental stages and milestones attained at each academic level. It allowed me to follow a group of children and learn from them while instructing reading and language arts from age four to age seven. It was an eye opening experience and provided me an exceptional foundation in which to formulate my ideas and philosophy about teaching children how to read.

What I discovered through my internships was that children who had been read to and stimulated intellectually as infants and toddlers came into the classroom willing, able and excited to read while those who perhaps weren't engaged to the same degree as their classmates were equally willing, less able and often lacked the confidence found in the students already possessing a solid language foundation.

After entering my own classroom which began with teaching Kindergarten, I decided that teaching children to read at the earliest possible age was key to providing children every opportunity available to them in life. My motto is, "If you can read you can do anything." I shared my philosophy with each group of students and the parents of every child I ever had the pleasure of instructing and these words inspired and motivated my students in ways beyond words. In fact, through utilization of teaching practices and tools that I designed to be used within my classroom, my first grade students were reading Nancy Drew & Hardy Boys novels in their entirety. It was a part of our everyday reading/rest-time procedure(s) in which I read aloud to the students while they took 20 minutes to listen and rest. This single event inspired a class full of students to become independent readers and begin reading the series on their own.

Teaching a child to read doesn't begin with letter recognition and sounds as some people will have you believe. It begins at a much more basic level and begins upon a child's birth. Below, I will identify the *Different Stages of Development* for children Birth to Age 7 as well as the literacy milestones attained at each stage. Keep in mind that no two children will acquire reading literacy as the same rate, but this guideline should assist you in recognizing the importance of teaching the fundamentals.

Pre-Reading Stage (Birth to Age Three)

Children will emulate their parents, caregivers and teachers during each stage of development.

Infants:

- Cooing and making babbling sounds as a form of communication and expression of happiness.
- Making sounds that imitate the tones and rhythms that adults use when communicating with them even completing words.
- Responding to facial gestures and expressions.
- Beginning to understand the meaning of spoken words and can associate words with objects, i.e. people, food, bottle, cup, blanket, etc...
- Playing games such as "peek-a-boo" and "pat-a-cake" which is demonstrative of games involving taking turns, repetition and song.
- Developing new ways to express basic needs, desires & feelings such as screaming, laughing, grunting and physical gestures like facial expressions and hand signals.

Toddlers:

- Learn to handle objects such as books (best if soft in composition) and blocks.
- Begin to recognize books by their covers and enjoy flipping through the pages reciting memorized stories, or creating their own stories as they point to words and/or pictures (pretending to read).
- Enjoy being read to & may even have a favorite book or two.
- Learning to understand "how" to handle books.
- Will be able to name some objects or characters within a story, i.e. Winnie the Pooh, Barney, etc...
- Will learn to identify pictures in books and make the connection that they are symbols for real things.
- Are capable of identifying specific letters found in text.
- Begin scribbling with a purpose in an effort to draw or write something.
- May begin to draw specific shapes and letters, i.e. the first letter of their name which they will also be able to identify in other forms of print.

Preschooler (Ages 3 & 4):

- Enjoy listening to and talking about books & stories.
- Understand that words in books are relaying meaning.
- Will attempt to read and write independently and with assistance, perhaps by reading to a doll, pet or sibling.
- Able to recognize environmental print, i.e. restaurant signs, stop signs, candy wrappers and cereal boxes.
- Will be able to recognize shapes, patterns and sequences in print.
- Enjoy participating in rhyming games such as songs, games, and nursery rhymes.
- Will be able to identify some, if not all, of the letters of the alphabet and might be able to produce the sounds of many.
- May be able to recognize and/or write his/her name.
- Some children may be able to write or attempt to write known letters to represent written language such as mom, dad, pet's and sibling names, etc...

Kindergarten:

By Kindergarten, many children will already be able to recite the alphabet, recognize the written letters and even identify many letter sounds. Some children will already be capable of writing their own name as well as other words. And some children will be capable of independent reading.

- Enjoy being read to by others.
- Uses expression in their voice when reading or pretending to read aloud and to others.
- Can retell stories including use of characters and settings.
- Use picture clues in an effort to read books.
- Will be able to use descriptive language to explain or ask questions pertaining to stories.
- Recognize the letters of the alphabet (both upper and lower case) and be able to identify the corresponding sounds.
- Capable of identifying and producing rhyming words.
- Able to demonstrate that print is read left to right and from top to bottom.
- Begin to match spoken words with written text.

- Will be able to recognize and read "high frequency" words used in text such as: a, the, but, that, are, than, I, etc...
- Capable of writing letters of the alphabet and words.
- Will begin to write stories.

First/Second Grade(s):

Reading / Decoding will become substantially more noticeable at this age meaning that children will be able to associate letters with their corresponding sounds using phonics to decode written words. There are a variety of reading methodologies that are used to teach reading another form being "sight" vocabulary which is recognizing "whole words" based upon context, pictures and word shape. It isn't uncommon for children at this age to focus on individual words often resulting in loss of the larger meaning of the story or sentence. Often at this stage in development children will be able to:

- Implement strategies to read unknown words (letter/sound relationships, context and word families).
- Easily decode phonetically.
- Able to identify a minimum of 100 high frequency words.
- Is capable of "self-correcting" mistakes made when reading aloud.
- Will be able to make reasonable predictions about stories that are unfamiliar based on story-plot, book titles and pictures.
- Are able to read and understand both fiction and non-fiction material.
- Should be able to retell a story including character names, description of the setting(s) and be able to identify problem(s) and solution(s) identified in the plot of the story.
- Will be capable of identifying the number of syllables in words.
- Can segment and blend sounds (individual phonemes) and "break" them to create other words.
- Be able to substitute, add or delete phonemes in words to make new words.

I have provided you the typical stages of development and developmental milestones that are associated within the age groups above. Please do not think that your child MUST be able to demonstrate each characteristic that I provided above nor should you believe that your child cannot exceed the capabilities as outlined.

Children are individuals and like snowflakes, each will be different including the ease at which they learn to read. It is a process and one that will occur naturally as they mature and develop. By providing your child the stimulation that he/she desires and needs from infancy throughout their developmental years, you will influence your child's rate of development in many ways. Case and point: My children received the same degree of stimulation as infants, however, my older son began speaking in ten word phrases and was capable of putting together complete thoughts, ideas and sentences by the time he was six months of age. My younger son, although just as capable, had most of his needs communicated for him by his older brother and therefore didn't choose to use his words until he was closer to ten months of age. Today, both are excellent readers and have been reading since before Kindergarten. One son is a phonetic speller/reader and can spell and read words that most adults struggle to read and /or spell. The other son reads for meaning and utilizes sight vocabulary and cannot spell some of the simplest words without assistance.

Children will let you know if they are ready to read through their actions and emotions. By acting upon your child's desire to "learn" things you can actually encourage them at a rate more developmentally appropriate. One-size does NOT fit all when it comes to the developmental capabilities of your children. Do what you feel comfortable doing in an effort to stimulate your child as long as the child responds in a positive manner. In other words, just because **YOU** may desire your child to be reading upon entrance into preschool and/or Kindergarten does not necessarily mean that your child is ready to read and you must respect their capabilities. Avoid frustrating your child in an effort to attain unrealistic goals.

So, if you take anything from this article it should be this. One day your child will learn to read. He/she may even take the lead. But for now the process may be slow. Just encourage them to watch and grow.

I have included several videos of children, some as young as sixteen months, reading with their parents. Each video is amazing in its own right. I encourage you to take this opportunity and watch the videos to see the potential your child has when it comes to learning to read.

http://www.youtube.com/watch?v=6maV5YYcLM8&feature=related

http://www.youtube.com/watch?v=PRdQCsPvxco&feature=related

http://www.youtube.com/watch?v=V5LlFkXfMZ8

The videos you just watched are utilizing specific learning programs geared for teaching your children how to read at incredibly young ages. You'll note that the children are eager and excited about the opportunity to learn and in fact one child becomes upset when her mother appears to be leaving the room prior to the lesson. I have reviewed both learning tools being used in the videos and found them to be innovative and easy to utilize when teaching your child. If you are looking for a product that anyone can use that makes teaching your child to read both creative and effective and which encompasses many different learning styles.

For information on the learning system used in the videos above, visit this link: http://www.brillkids.com/

Recipe for Kids Play Clay

Young children enjoy playing with many different things from race cars to baby dolls and pretty much everything in between. But sometimes, children bore of certain toys or items as they've exhausted, if only for a short while, their ability to "get creative" with them. I'm talking about lots of different manipulatives such as blocks, puzzles, and even certain crafty items. There is one type of "toy" or "manipulative" that children always seem to enjoy - play dough, silly putty, or clay. It seems that no matter how many times this type of manipulative is introduced to children, they light up and immediately begin creating.

It is truly one item that children will not easily bore. In fact, teachers use it extensively in the classroom as it provides a creative way for teaching shapes, colors, letters, numbers, and many other cognitive skills. It is also excellent for tactile stimulation as it allows children to use their vocabulary to describe what they are feeling, in terms of textures, explain "what" they are making, and certainly it will elicit a great deal of conversation among

friends. The problem with "clay" or "play dough" is that it can get expensive, dries quickly if left exposed to air, and gets dirty. So, in order to become thrifty in the classroom, or at home, many teachers and parents make their own. Today's marvelous masterpiece is homemade kids play clay.

Marvelous Masterpiece - Kids Play Clay

What you'll need:

- 1 cup table salt (not sea salt or rock salt)
- 1/3 cup water
- 1/2 cup Clabber Girl Cornstarch (or another brand)
- 1/4 cup cold water
- Food Coloring (this item is optional but certainly allows for more fun in designing)
- medium saucepan
- metal spoon
- cookie sheet or a vinyl place mat
- vinyl or plastic table cloth or solid surface (not wooden or tile)
- cookie cutters
- rolling pin
- plastic knives, forks, spoons

After you've gotten all of your necessary supplies together, the rest is actually really easy. If your children are old enough, allow them to assist you in creating the clay. They'll enjoy it - it's a wonderful opportunity to teach them about measurements, and a fun activity for them to participate.

Steps to Follow:

1. In a medium saucepan, mix salt and 1/3 cup of water over medium heat, stirring occasionally (about 3 to 4 minutes).
2. Remove mixture from the heat; add cornstarch, and 1/4 cup of cold water.
3. Add a few drops of food coloring, if desired.
4. The mixture will resemble mashed potatoes. Stir until it thickens, cool, and then knead of a cookie sheet, vinyl place mat, or solid surface lightly dusted with cornstarch to help prevent it from sticking.

That's all there is to it. Kids Play Clay can be stored in the refrigerator in a sealed container with a damp sponge or paper towel to maintain the level of moisture. It is so easy to make, it is often wise to make several batches in different colors. Children will enjoy hours of fun entertaining themselves with this super easy manipulative.

Restaurant Etiquette for Children & Families

Although we all come from different places, backgrounds and probably differ on a vast number of ethical, moral, religious and political views, there is one thing that most of us can probably agree upon.....restaurant etiquette. Yes, I'm pretty sure most of us will agree, when sitting in a restaurant trying to enjoy an overpriced meal (which they all are) the last thing(s) that we want to deal with is our meal being interrupted by a misbehaving child. In fact, I'll bet you are not alone in wishing that the parent of the disruptive child would do something about him/her to allow the childless patrons to enjoy their evening meal, lunch and/or breakfast and prevent those with children from watching and learning from other misbehaving children.

Sadly it seems, and more often than not, parents of children that become disruptive in restaurants think they can simply wait it out and the child will eventually succumb to their demands. What is sadder is that these parents have very little concern about the impact of their child's behavior on the other patrons attempting to enjoy themselves.

I understand that everyone deserves a meal out including parents of the disruptive child but it shouldn't come at the expense of others. Unfortunately for the parents, "their" child may disturb their dinner plans but the child shouldn't be allowed to disrupt the plans of countless   others.

Although there are many, here are a list of the top ten disruptive behaviors needing immediate attention and correction by parents:

Ten Behaviors Inappropriate in a Restaurant:

1. the screaming child;
2. the child jumping up and down in the booth or chair;
3. the parent screaming repeatedly at the child to settle down;
4. the child throwing his/her food (which consequently lands in the middle of yours;

5. the child running up and down the isles;
6. the child with the odorous diaper;
7. the child fighting with his/her sibling;
8. the child who's I-Pod or video game is loud enough for you to hear at the next table;
9. the child who continues to throw his/her bottle, pacifier, rattle, teething ring over the booth or into your area;
10. The parent that refuses to excuse him/herself along with the child that is disturbing others from enjoying their meal at the restaurant!!!

Each of these behaviors and more is the responsibility of the parent and should be handled immediately and in a fashion so as not to disturb others. For example, the child that continues to bounce, jump, and hit the seat while confined to a booth is more likely than not disturbing the patron on the other side. It should NOT be the responsibility of the disturbed patron to have to identify the disturbance and ask the parents to make the child stop!

Additionally, the parent that sounds like a parrot asking, telling, demanding and threatening the child in an effort to "make them" stop a particular behavior is just as annoying as the behavior that the child is practicing. In fact it's a toss-up as to which behavior is more annoying.

We recently visited a local restaurant to celebrate a special occasion. The restaurant is a little more expensive than others in the area but not something outlandish and the perfect atmosphere for enjoying an evening out. No sooner were we seated at a table than a mother and two children arrived. Immediately after placing our order it began. The youngest child began to whine, then cry, then scream and basically disrupt the evening for everyone sitting in the front portion of the restaurant.

Upon scanning the patrons, people were agitated and irritated. They were rolling their eyes and notably the topic of discussion was the inability or lack of concern that the mother had for anyone other than her own appetite. Finally, the restaurant manager, who'd, been made of aware of the situation by several patrons, asked her to remove the child. Angered by the request, she refused until further prompted when the second child began to chime in with crying and the addition of a temper tantrum.

Teaching children restaurant etiquette should be something that **all** parents do before visiting a restaurant. It shouldn't wait until the child has managed to ruin the evening for other patrons. If a child is unable to remain in his/her seat, eating the food that is served without throwing it, yelling, screaming, and basically acting like a menace, it is probably wise to either leave the kids at home OR teach them how to behave in the presence of others.

Restaurant etiquette isn't just for children either. Believe it or not there are many adults that are clueless to the types of behaviors that they need to leave at the door upon entering a restaurant. For instance, the sudden urge to "get jiggy with it" is better if NOT in the presence of children and other patrons dining in a restaurant. You've heard the saying, "Get a room" or perhaps go home!

Additionally, adults who think the entire restaurant full of patrons wants to HEAR them rant and rave about their ex-spouse, their terrible boss and/or job, their cellphone conversations, their conversations with other friends amongst the dinner party who believe that they are the only people in the restaurant, or that they refuse to pay for the food they ordered because they ordered the wrong thing. Exercise good judgment as the dining experience isn't just about your enjoyment but that of others too.

What to Do in the Event of a Disturbance:

Knowing when to say something and when to keep silent is a big one. You can either sit through your meal listening to the child screaming and yelling or you can do something about it. Most restaurant managers will handle the matter without your insistence, however, there may be a time when you've had enough and are at wits end and management needs a little prodding. You can either:

1. Notify your waitress/waiter to the matter and allow them to take the necessary steps to handle it;
2. Excuse yourself from the table and address the matter yourself with the manager;
3. Speak to the parents of the child that is being disruptive. It all depends on the comfort level that you have when it comes to "speaking up" for yourself and others.
4. Should the disturbance be an adult, you'll want to weigh your options as we know; often time's disruptions can be elevated due to the consumption of alcohol. If you don't feel comfortable handling the matter yourself, seek management. If

management is unsuccessful in handling the matter, you still have options. Either request another seat in the restaurant away from the party that is disruptive or leave the restaurant, perhaps indicating that due to management's inability to handle the matter, a reduced price or perhaps a complimentary meal is in order.

5. Finally, depending upon the situation, contact the authorities. Believe it or not, this is sometimes the only way to handle certain situations (usually not involving children) but adults that are out of line or control. I recently witnessed a lady that ordered her meal over the phone. Upon arriving to pick up her order she noticed that she'd ordered incorrectly and refused to pay for the incorrect item she'd ordered. Oh, she admitted that she'd ordered in error BUT that anywhere in America if you didn't like it you didn't pay for it or you could get your money back. One hour later she was still at it. The authorities were finally summoned and she was escorted out of the restaurant with her bag of "cold" food. Was it really worth it?

Teaching Table Manners:

In the hustle and bustle of life, many families rarely sit down to the table to eat a meal together at home. Many families are catching a bite at fast food restaurants while others simply drive-thru and consume their meals in the car while driving from Point A to Point B. It's ridiculous to think that we've allowed our schedules, and those of our children, to become so busy that we can't take an hour to sit down and enjoy a meal together. Now this is not to say that everyone lives this hectic lifestyle, nor is it to say that families NEVER sit down to eat together. It is the case of many which is also a major contributor to the increase in childhood obesity (and adult obesity as well).

As parents, we should make it a point to schedule a minimum of one hour each evening to allow the family to sit down at a table and eat. Research has proven that families that eat a meal together have better relationships; children have better grades; and children of these families are less likely to use drugs or practice unsafe or unhealthy lifestyles.

It's a simple as marking family dinner on a calendar and blocking that one hour for family dinner without television, video gaming, friends, etc....; planning a menu in advance that you can prepare (with the help of your family) so that a healthy meal is served; and then working together to practice table manners and etiquette. The same etiquette that you'd expect a child to practice when at a restaurant, at a friend's house, or wherever he/she may enjoy a meal outside of your own home.

Getting back to basics and living for one hour a day like times in the past when families gathered for meals is a vital part of family development. It is a time when we teach one another the importance of eating healthy, how to use good table etiquette and manners and more importantly, engage in meaningful conversations with our loved ones.

Perhaps if everyone made it a point, if not every evening, but perhaps twice or three times a week, restaurant etiquette would be less of an issue than it is today. I, for one, would love to go out to dinner for an evening free from the distractions of the child running up and down the aisle knocking beverages off other patrons table or the ability to enjoy the live music without the frequent and annoying vocal outbursts of the dad yelling at his child.

Teach your child basic table manners. In time, additional manners which will require teaching will be easier and more attainable even for the youngest child.

CHAPTER NINETEEN

WHAT BEGINS WITH THE LETTER "S"?

Keeping Your Children Safe – Child Abductions are Serious Offences

Last week, I saw a post on Facebook about a young child who was suspected to have been abducted and whose mother was reported murdered. This story scared me and made me increasingly aware of how precious our children are and how "at-risk" they can be when left unattended. Child abductions in the United States are staggering. In fact, there are more than 4500 children thought abducted and missing in our country. Although this story continues to be updated, and details modified, the fact is that the 6-year old boy is still unaccounted for. Family and friends do not know of his whereabouts and that results in much family strife. If you are a parent, plan to become a parent or have ever lost a child to any circumstance, you'll want to pay particular attention to this article. I thank the individual for posting the article and helping to bring awareness to such a devastating event.

With summer on the horizon, the number of children who will be left at home alone is also staggering. It is reported that between five and seven million children between the ages of five to thirteen will be left unattended for some portion of the day (or night). This is alarming when you consider the number of child abductions that take place annually. Not to mention that it is illegal to leave children under the age of twelve at home alone. Every day in the United States, approximately two children are abducted. Many times these abductions could have been prevented.

If you're one of the parents who feels that they DON'T have a choice but to leave their children at home alone or unattended, you may want to review the statistics below. It just may motivate you to make arrangements for your child and his/her safety.

Statistics of Child Abductions:

Each year, in the United States alone, more than 800,000 children are reported missing. Now, of these alarmingly high numbers, some are simply children who've remained out past their curfew or extended a visit at a non-custodial parent's home without notification resulting in the other parent filing a report. Better to be safe than sorry? Trust me I understand this fear and how devastating a parent feels when a child is not where he/she is supposed to be at a certain hour.

The truth is, the numbers are frightening and parents should be alarmed and concerned. Let me share 2010's abduction statistics:

- Of the 800,000 reported child abductions each year in the United States, 350,000 are family abductions related to violations of custody arrangements;
- There are actually 260,000 abducted annually;
- 204,000 are non-family abductions;
- 115 of these abductions end with serious injury or death to the child.

Of the reported abductions, on average 115 is considered non-family abductions and are categorized as stereotypical abductions. What is a stereotypical abduction?

Stereotypical Abductions:

Stereotypical abductions meet the following criteria:

- The victim is detained overnight;
- Transported more than 50 miles from home;
- Held for ransom;
- Intended to keep permanently or to kill.
- 40% are killed;
- 4% are never found;
- 79% are abducted by strangers;
- 21% are abducted by an acquaintance.

The danger of abductions doesn't always end up in death. Fortunately, yet unfortunately for many children, physical and emotional harm is often the end result which often leaves a survivor with many psychological scars to learn to cope with. These statistics are sad and often unforgivable. Out-of-family abductions are serious and something that can be avoided.

Out of Family Abductions:

Now, this doesn't mean that the abductor is NOT an acquaintance - it simply means that there is "no" biological attachment to the victim. Statistics of this type of abduction deserves your attention.

- 16% are left with severe mental harm / scars;
- 8% are physically abused;
- 7% are sexually violated and abused;
- 46% are female abductors;
- 54% are male abductors;

The next type of abduction is categorized as Non-Family abductions and these are the most brutal of the abductions.

Non-Family Abductions:

- 65% are young females;
- 46% are sexually assaulted/violated/abused;
- 31% are physically abused and/or harmed;
- 32% are street and/or car abductions with 25% of these victims being taken from wooded areas or parked/idling automobiles.

The three most common places for abducted and imprisoned children to be kept are:

1. Abductors automobile;
2. Abductors home/residence;
3. Abductors building (apartment/place of business).

Since abductions can be prevented with simple precautionary measures and education, it is important to understand or recognize the "truths" about abductions.

Abductors are most often male (75%). Most abductions take place 1/4 mile from a child's home which means often within a child's allowable play parameter. Of the male abductors, 67% are below the age of 29 years of age which may not raise the suspicion of a child being targeted.

There are many things that you can do to protect your children. Some will involve what YOU need to do to be prepared in the event of a missing child; and some of the suggestions will assist you in preparing your children so that they can avoid crossing paths with a child abductor.

Let's begin with proactive measures that can be taken to help you protect your children from the threat of falling victim to preventable crimes.

- **<u>Stranger Danger</u>** - I know you've heard of it and it is something that your children should be familiar with too. Teach your children beginning at an early age how to be cautious around others. You'll want to teach them how to maintain safety around all other(s) in all types of environments. Here is a link to assist you in providing the proper details when teaching your children.

  http://www.mychildsafety.net/stranger-danger.html
- **<u>Safe Environments</u>** - Children should be taught which environments are safe and which are not. This includes areas in which they socialize with others; engage in play and/or sporting events; the neighborhood in which you live; and paths traveled to and from school, the library, the bus or any location that you deem appropriate or necessary.
- **<u>Inappropriate Contact</u>** - Even though we cringe at the thought, children need to be taught about inappropriate touching or physical contact. This is not to say that we want to hyper-intensify this topic as there have been many cases in which parents have been wrongfully accused, but we do want to help them learn to differentiate between "good" and "bad" touches/contact.
- **<u>Teaching Children how to Recognize Details</u>** - As "random" as this may sound, it is helpful to teach our children how to "identify" certain characteristics and details so that in the event it ever becomes necessary, they can provide details about individuals that they consider suspect/dangerous. Helping children identify things such as facial details like bushy eyebrows, scar on cheek (left side, right side, chin or forehead) face, birthmark, etc....; blonde, brown, red or black hair; eye color; heavy, medium, or light weight - body type; male or female; young or old; tall or

short. These types of characteristics are beneficial in the event that a playmate, sibling or individual is witnessed being taken against his/her will.

- **Sensing Danger** *(Profiling)* - This is something like "profiling" but it necessary in today's society. With two children abducted every day, it is important that children learn how to "feel" when they sense possible danger. For instance, a child should be able to recognize (in advance) the dangers associated with a car pulling up to them on their way home and offering them a ride; an individual at the door asking if they can borrow the telephone or "pretending" to sell something; or even a person approaching them at the playground or park asking for assistance in "catching" or finding their lost dog. Call it what you want to - but profiling has saved many lives.

- **What to Do IF** - Children need to be taught what to do in the event of an emergency or simply in times of fear or uncertainty. For instance, children should be taught "what" and "how" to answer the door (or not) if a parent is unavailable; children need to be taught phone etiquette and what to say if a parent is unavailable; there need to be clear instructions about entering an empty home (after school) should they arrive home before you are present; they need to be taught how to secure the home if they are home alone (lock the front door, ensure the garage door is closed, etc...); children must be taught how to obtain assistance should there be a problem - a fire; burglary; home invasion; sick pet; ill sibling; poison control; who to call in the event of this or that (numbers should be posted); every home should have a safety zone - a place where a child can "hide" if he/she feels threatened and how to seek assistance if he/she is injured; a hard-wired telephone - wireless phones go dead and that can be costly in the event of an emergency; lastly, a close neighbor or relative that is ALWAYS available if a child must be self-sufficient and alone at any point in time. Every home should have posted telephone numbers for: Parent's Work Numbers and Cellphone Numbers; Neighbor; Local Police Department; Sheriff Department; Poison Control; Animal Control; Fire Department (911); CDC; Relatives; Friends of Children; Doctor; Hospital; and other specific Emergency Services within your Community.

For parent(s), grandparents, and caregivers, being prepared is also paramount in the event that the unimaginable occurs. There are certain things that everyone should do to protect themselves and their loved ones. Teaching your children these tips and making certain that everything is in place is important. Otherwise, you'll be unprepared in the event of an emergency.

Tips and Suggestions to keep Your Children Safe:

- For younger children, label everything. From clothing, jackets, backpacks or sports equipment, labels will help to provide evidence should your child ever be missing.
- Older children should carry some form of identification - a school identification card; driver's license; state issued identification card.
- Telephones (cell phones) have GPS tracking capabilities. My children carry a cellphone for the express purpose of me knowing where they are at all times. If they are ever late, I simply "track" their whereabouts and receive a text message or email immediately identifying their location on a map. They also have devices for younger children that can be attached to a book bag, shoelace, jacket, etc....
- Medical bracelets should be provided and worn by any child with information that could help to prevent injury or death.
- Fingerprinting, DNA, and dental records are also a wonderful tool to have "just in case" a child should be lost. Although difficult to think about, it is definitely worth it in the event that you ever have to identify a child.
- Up to date photograph, height, weight, eye color, distinctive marks or scars, medical records (missing appendix, tonsils, etc...) and relevant information that will help professionals identify or assist in posting information about a missing child - Amber Alerts, etc.... (Ideally, photographs should be updated every 3 months to ensure that it is an accurate depiction of the child - they grow so fast.
- Parents should obtain up-to-date phone numbers of their children's closet friends in order to have a place to start in the event that a child doesn't come home. It's also wise to get to know your child's friends, their families and establish a community of concerned parents and citizens.
- Knowing who, what, when and where your children are at all times is the best way to keep up with them; however, knowing children (especially teenagers), this often easier said than done. Explaining the dangers associated with freedom is important so that your children will understand the necessity of keeping you informed of their whereabouts (ahead of time).

- Establishing curfews are extremely important and enforcing them in order to make them effective.
- Automobiles can also be equipped with tracking devices so that you'll always know where your child's vehicle is or perhaps where your child was last. This is a great feature in the event of a carjacking situation.
- Alternative contact(s) are a wonderful mechanism if your teenager is afraid to contact you in the event of an accident, emergency or need for assistance (intoxication, sexual misconduct, legal infarction). This should be established if there is any discontent within your relationship with your child.

These are just a few suggestions to assist you in educating and preparing your child or children for anything out of the ordinary. By taking these steps, you can hopefully ward off the possibility of your child becoming harmed or taken against his/her will. It will also provide you the tools needed to secure his/her safe return with the assistance of your community and legal professionals.

Keep your children safe. Please don't wait until it's too late!

The Importance of Sensory Learning

If you are a teacher you know what is meant when someone refers to a sensory table, sensory learning or perhaps even a *discovery table*. If you aren't, this concept or term may be unfamiliar to you. For purposes of this article, we will refer to sensory experiences by using the phrase "sensory table".

Sensory/Tactile Learning:

Sensory learning is extremely important in childhood developmental since children learn through the use of each of their senses. It focuses on tactile stimulation, or sense of touch, providing a medium from which learning about the environment is made possible.

Most classrooms, especially at the preschool level through 1st or 2nd grades have sensory tables. So what is a sensory table? It can be any type of container filled with some type of tactile medium. By allowing children to experiment with many types and varieties of textures, they are able to improve and/or increase their development of fine motor skills. Fine motor skills are important as it allows children to manipulate toys and using utensils such as spoons, forks, crayons, paintbrushes and even a toothbrush. Additionally,

by allowing an opportunity for children to enhance their fine motor skills they will be better able to complete simple tasks for themselves such as self-help tasks like getting dressed, tying their shoes, brushing or combing their hair and more. The more exposure and experience children have to fine motor building the more capable and better foundation they'll have for meeting classroom expectations in handwriting.

Other Developmental Areas:

Not only will children improve their fine motor skills when working with sensory tables, they'll also develop other areas such as learning and understand concepts such as "on/off", "big/little", and "in/out". Additionally, working cooperatively with others at sensory table children will develop social skills as they engage in social interaction among their peers.

Items Used In Sensory Table(s):

There are hundreds of items that can be used in sensory tables most of which you can obtain from your pantry or the local grocery store. Below is a list of commonly used items. **Note**: Keep in mind the ages of the children using the table as you want to ensure that you aren't providing items that will be placed within their mouth. Sensory tables can get messy. You might want to consider a location that won't destroy your carpet or flooring.

Sensory Table Ingredients:

- Cheerios with spoons and bowls
- Oatmeal
- Beans
- Rice
- Leaves (make certain they aren't poisonous)
- Nuts (consider children with nut allergies)
- Sand
- Water
- Grass

- Dry Pasta Noodles
- Ice Cubes in Sand
- Colored Curling Ribbon cut into Small Pieces
- Flour or cornmeal
- Coffee grinds (unused)
- Flubber (Elmer's glue mixed with liquid starch)
- Ublek (equal parts cornstarch and water) melts in your hands (add food color)
- Rice (colored with liquid watercolors or Wilton's food coloring)
- Deer corn with black beans or rocks to grind the corn

Additional Manipulatives include:

- Scooping tools (spoons, measuring cups, ice cream scoop)
- Buckets & bowls
- Plastic Bugs, Fish or Other creatures (especially if theme teaching)
- Turkey Basters (when using liquids)
- Clothespins
- Kitchen Sifter
- Funnels
- Spatula
- Egg Carton(s) for sorting
- Cups
- Manual Egg Beaters
- Whisks
- Containers w/lids

How often should Sensory Table materials be Switched:

This is often dependent upon the children. If they are still actively engaged, learning and enjoying discovering, leave it there. If the children have bored of its contents and tend to be doing other "unacceptable" things, it's a good time to change the contents.

Building a Sensory Table:

Anyone can build a sensory table using a variety of materials. For example, visiting your local department store you'll be able to find a wide variety of plastic tubs and containers of different depths and side-heights. You'll want to choose one that is approximately 6 to 8 inches in height to allow children to easily access the contents. I found that the larger the dimensions, i.e. 24" x 36", more children can use the table together.

You can either set the "sensory table" upon a table such as an outdoor picnic table (depending upon the weather & outdoor conditions) or inside an area where the flooring is conducive to the contents of the table.

Some tables have their own frame which can be constructed by using plumbing pipes configured to provide support for the tub itself as well as to provide legs enabling the table to be free-standing. You can also use wood, as long as you are careful to sand the edges or countersink the nails or screws to avoid unnecessary scrapes to the children.

I've seen plastic kiddie pools also used as sensory tables - especially when studying themes within a classroom. Within the pool was sand & water, or bubbles with different shaped objects to allow for creating bubbles, etc...

Be creative - after all, it is something that will provide hours of creative entertainment for your children and most of all, enjoy.

Teaching Good Sportsmanship

Instilling good sportsmanship within our children is becoming increasingly more difficult with the overabundance of multimedia messages spouting "winning is everything" every time we turn on the television to watch a sporting event or attend live events. Add to it the outrageous, and much publicized behavior(s) of professional athletes, i.e. trash-talk, violence, use of illegal performance enhancing drugs, bribes, spousal abuse, etc....and you've set the stage for poor sportsmanship across the board. And, no matter how we encourage our children to emulate athletes' representative of good sportsmanship, moral fortitude and upstanding character, they will always be influenced by the behavior of ALL professional athletes, good and bad.

Many of you probably watched or heard about the 2006 comedy Talladega Nights in which Ricky Bobby (played by Will Ferrell), a race car driver quotes a lesson that he'd learned from his dad when only a small child, "If you ain't first, you're last!" In the movie this line was absolutely hilarious, especially when followed by his father's response, "That doesn't

make any sense at all, you can be second, third, or fourth.....you can even be fifth!" The point is, whatever happened to teaching children the old adage, "It's not whether you win or lose, but how you play the game that's important"?

My family has been very fortunate over the years having excellent coaches in most of the sports that my children have been involved. I have two very athletically gifted sons who've played sports since the age of three. They've played baseball, soccer, football, basketball, tennis and golf. They've run track, participated on swim teams, been involved in gymnastics and have competed in Triathlons. We've had wonderful coaches who were concerned about teaching the children "how" to play the sport in which they were involved, modeled exceptional sportsmanship and **NEVER** raised their voice at any member of the team. On the flip side, and unfortunately more common than not, we've had a coach or two that believed that winning was the only option; focused more on drilling the kids and only involved the "better" athletes on the team; and to top it off, *yelled, ranted and raved* not just during practice(s) but while engaged in sporting competitions against other teams. Embarrassing - you bet! Frustrating - beyond words! Acceptable - absolutely not!

When I've been witness to coaches such as the coaches practicing what I consider to be inappropriate, unprofessional and certainly demoralizing behaviors to children, I had to ask myself: "Is this the sporting atmosphere that I want my children involved?" My answer was "no" and I immediately took action to correct the situation(s) not just for the exposure that my children were suffering but for the other children as well whose parents didn't exercise their voices to correct the problem (other than complaining amongst themselves at each practice or game).

So, how do we ensure that our children are involved in sports or other activities demonstrating a positive team atmosphere modeling good sportsmanship qualities....Both parents and coaches can start by focusing on a few simple issues.

1. ***Focus on Sportsmanship.*** First and foremost, by stepping onto the field encouraging children to embrace, "It's not whether you win or lose, but how you play the game that's important" you'll actually be instilling in our children that champions are made from something they have deep inside them -- a desire, a dream, and a vision. You'll be teaching them valuable character building-blocks that

will inspire children to become compassionate, caring, good team players - after all, there is no "I" in TEAM. When you think about the parallels sports have to life in general, you should consider that the character children gain from involvement in athletics carries over into their everyday perceptions of and attitudes in life. (Just look at  John McEnroe - phenomenal tennis player, promoted equal pay for both men and women players but a terrible role model when it came to good sportsmanship qualities). When they develop the attitude that their involvement on a team is all about winning the MVP at the end of the season instead of instilling the desire to share collectively the victories among the team, you've basically created a very self-absorbed/centered, "me" first individual. I cannot think of a better example of an athlete who cared more about the team collectively and taking them ALL to victory than Tim Tebow. He represented what good sportsmanship is all about.

2. ***Be a Proper Role Model:*** When involved in sporting events, keep in mind that your representation on and/or off the field will certainly get noticed not just by children but by other parents. By offering praise and providing encouragement to ALL players on the field, even the opponents, you are setting an example that I'd like to think all parents would want their children to emulate. Berating, criticizing and condemning children, coaches (umpires, officials and referees) on your child's team or on opposing teams is counter-productive when it comes to good sportsmanship. Behave like an adult and realize that EVERY child and adult on the team (or field) deserves encouragement, respect and words of kindness. Every child participating has a desire to do the best he/she can do and certainly is giving it everything they've got. So what if they miss the game winning field goal, or cannot make the basket to tie the game....they've done their best and their efforts should be recognized and praised. Encouragement will pave the way to future successes. Good deeds, sportsmanship and conduct are contagious. Make it count and help encourage and promote positive behaviors by others. Note: If you have a problem with something that was handled inappropriately, don't reciprocate and handle it inappropriately too. Wait until the time is right and address the matter privately or at least out of earshot of others.

3. ***Focus and Personal Gratification:*** A child's involvement in sports should ultimately be about a child's desire to be involved in the activity in order to perform

to their best ability and gain something positive from the experience. Any involvement in sports or extracurricular activities should be about providing children with a pleasurable, social experience in order to encourage a better sense of self-worth, skills and sportsmanship. (It can be about encouraging and providing opportunities for safer, healthier social engagements too). It should NOT be about a parent's desire to use his/her child's sports accomplishments for ulterior purposes such as collegiate scholarships, reliving their own sports days vicariously through the child, bragging rights or perhaps their future retirement.

4. *Promote The Golden Rule*: Watching and learning while attending or participating in sporting events or simply watching them on television is the perfect opportunity for finding "teachable moments" when it comes to good AND bad sportsmanship alike. As mentioned before, there are many ill-behaved players and coaches these days that for whatever reason find opportunities to showboat taunt their opponents and even treat the officials and/or other players with incredible levels of contempt and disrespect. By taking advantage of these "teachable moments" through open-ended questions to assess your child's opinions or thoughts about the "event" taking place, you'll have the opportunity to 1) listen to your child's ideas or opinions about what has been witnessed both on and off the field without sounding like you're lecturing; 2) offer suggestions about treating other participants and/or officials the way that they would want to be treated. The perfect time to be able to promote good sportsmanship.

5. *Evaluating Coaches who Embrace Good Sportsmanship*: As difficult as it is for coaches to go into coaching without the mindset of "WIN - WIN - WIN" because we've been taught to embrace the "Everybody Loves a Winner" mentality, it is important to remember that winning isn't the only purpose for children being there. In fact, many families involve their children in sports and athletics to encourage sportsmanship, team building, socialization and involvement in structured activities. So, what message is being sent about good sportsmanship when we see coaches such as the late Woody Hayes attacking the opposing team's Linebacker; or Bobby Knight throwing a chair across the basketball court, or even Steve Spurrier throwing his headset onto the ground destroying it? Coaches should nurture good sportsmanship and should remember parents' values regarding what good sportsmanship is all about as it should be his/her core goal in working with kids. Additionally, coaches need to remember that good sportsmanship includes a TEAM which defined means EVERY member and not just those that coaches have

deemed more talented resulting in a guaranteed victory on the field, court or ring. Victories are found both on and off the field. Coaching children is a privilege and an honor that parents provide when encouraging and enrolling children to participate in sports. It carries both a moral responsibility to contribute to the healthy character development of young athletes and facilitates allowing each player to try his/her best which is the ultimate definition of success. Good sportsmanship is taught best when everyone on the team is provided equal representation, every day. Nothing deters more from maintaining a positive attitude, good sportsmanship or the ability to feel genuinely enthusiastic and as a member of a TEAM than being present but not being included. Having been a former educator, soccer coach and athlete, recognizing that good sportsmanship and building/establishing interpersonal relationships is dependent upon a sense of comradery among teammates and/or classmates. Encouraging comradery among teammates involves inclusion on the field, court, or activity venue and not just being left on the bench or sideline as a spectator. Jealousy (and insecurity) rears its ugly head promoting negative thoughts, words and actions that ultimately come into play. Unfortunately, it is due to jealousy that bad sportsmanship, showboating, and other inappropriate attitudes and behaviors are becoming more and more prevalent both on and off the field.

Teaching good sportsmanship involves many aspects, many of which we may not recognize. With attitudes such as *"You don't WIN silver or " You LOSE gold"* being promoted in the media during the 1996 summer Olympics, or as funny as it sounds, *"If you ain't first, you're last"*, it has become more difficult to teach children the real reason that we learn, play and/or become involved in sports and activities. With the entire focus being on "winning" we lose the bigger and more important focus which should be about a child's intrinsic desire to participate, the skills and personal achievements gained and the basic need to be a part of a group and valued member of that group while establishing comradery. Attitude is everything and having a positive attitude is more easily accomplished and practiced both on and off the field when you are both an active and valued member of the team. (Bench warmers often feel dejected and like a lessor member of the team. Facial expressions and body posture/mannerisms say it all.)

Sidebar: We've all heard the saying, *"practice makes perfect."* Just like in the classroom where students must practice and practice in order to learn a new academic skill, athletes must be granted the same opportunity. In other words, they enter sports with a dream and desire to

be the best football, baseball, soccer, tennis, etc....player there ever was. Some players will be naturally gifted athletes and excel over the others - BUT, should this mean that the player(s) who already have the skills and talents be the only player(s) to receive the undivided attention of the coaches? Absolutely not! There are just as many gifted and talented children sitting on the benches awaiting their turn to shine and be noticed if only given the opportunity to learn and improve. Good sportsmanship begins here!!! In the classroom would you focus only on the child that already understands and has mastered the skill(s) and concepts being taught? Absolutely not, so why would it be any different in athletics?

For video clips on inappropriate sportsmanship, click on the links below. You'll be amazed at some of the activities that unfortunately have been promoted as acceptable, although penalized on the field or court that children are exposed to during media coverage of sporting events.

http://www.poetv.com/video.php?vid=29397the late Coach Woody Hayes

http://www.youtube.com/watch?v=NvRO2GE4x4M_ Coach Bobby Knight

http://www.youtube.com/watch?v=o3Kbc-LSGvI&feature=related
Top 10 Angry Moments in Sports (Unsportsmanlike Conduct)

Spring is in the Air - Planting Activity

This mini-activity will focus around planting flowers for everyone's delight. Even if your children are older, they'll be able to assist in preparing the soil and planting beautiful, fragrant flowers to make any landscape lovely.

Let's Begin:

Teaching children about plants is a fun activity as you can't look out the window without seeing something growing. But, what's most interesting is showing them the seeds from which plants originate. This activity will allow children to observe the different types of plant seeds, their color(s), shapes, and sizes and then allow them to see the plants that will actually sprout from each seed planted. We'll also focus on the (3) things that all plants must have in order to grow and thrive: water, sunlight, and good soil.

- **First**, take a visit to a local seed store (Lowes, Home Depot, even Target) and choose from a variety of plant seeds. If you desire flowers that will come back each year you'll choose perennial; if you simply want flowers to bloom for the course of a season and not return next year, you'll choose annuals. You can explain this concept by letting children know that perennial plants will become dormant (sleep) through the winter like a hibernating bear and annuals will perish much like a butterfly at the end of its life cycle.
- **Second**, once you've chosen the seeds you're going to plant, allow the children to observe each seed. Some will be large like a whole black pepper clove; while others will be smaller than a grain of salt. Some will be dark colored, while some will be colorful with specks on them. I'd recommend finding a container with multiple compartments such as a container used for separating pills taken daily (weekly), or perhaps a container used for separating fish hooks/lures. This portion of the lesson will allow you to focus on vocabulary words such as adjectives (describing words) which each child can use as they tell what they see when they observe each seed.
- **Third** activity will be to show your children the flowers that will grow from each seed. This is fun activity as some of the largest blooming flowers will actually come from the tiniest seed and vice versa.
- **Finally**, using Peat Pods, have the children germinate their seeds by first soaking the pods in water to allow them to expand. Then, sprinkle a seed or three into the pod so that it can begin the germinating process. When planting seeds, usually the seedlings are pretty frail so I've found that germinating within a pod inside a plastic "greenhouse" is a great way to get a healthy plant. After the plants have sprouted and are between 4 - 6 inches tall, you can transplant them into a garden or larger pot (depending upon the growth instructions on the seed packet.

Note: If you'd prefer, you can actually germinate the seeds inside a zip lock bag with a moist paper towel folded around the seeds. This provides the warmth needed to germinate along with the moisture (that won't escape). You can place the bag in a window or outside. Keep in mind that you'll want the seeds to have a portion of the day in the shade so that they don't cook within the bag. Once the seed sprouts, you'll want to transplant them. A great experiment when teaching children about seeds, plants and what they require to grow is to place the seed in the wet paper towel and then inside a zip lock bag. Place one bag where it receives ample daylight and another inside a dark cabinet. Check them daily and allow the children to review and compare what the seeds have done.

Enjoy this exciting activity with your children which may, in fact, become planting a vegetable garden that you can harvest for healthy, organic eating.

CHAPTER TWENTY

WHAT BEGINS WITH THE LETTER "T"?

Teenage Fashion Do's & Don'ts for Guys

Guys, guys, guys - Why? Why? Why do you leave the house looking like you climbed out of your bed having spent the night in the clothes that you're wearing to school? Why do you let your hair look like your dog does after rolling around in a pile of something in the backyard? Is this REALLY how you're hoping to impress for success?

While girls may *pretend* to like what you're selling (the way you look), that is exactly what they are doing - they're pretending. They do this in order to maintain your attention. Let me ask you, how many of you guys would find a girl attractive that looked as though she'd climbed right out of bed, walked out the door and arrived at school in this manner? No makeup, no general hygiene considerations, nothing done to the hair - except maybe a baseball cap of sorts placed on top, etc....I think you get the point or at least I hope you do. Well, guess what...girls aren't particularly impressed with your style or lack thereof either.

Whatever happened to wanting to look nice? Sadly, with most teens it seems to be a thing of the past. It doesn't have to be and it certainly should not. Girls prefer guys who demonstrate good hygiene. They like guys that have fresh breath, pearly white teeth, a nice complexion, neat hair and well-manicured nails. And believe me when I say that these "traits" aren't just noticed by the older generation. Girls, as young as second grade who have begun to notice "boys" look for these things and discuss them with their friends. It doesn't end there either. "Looking", just as with boys, is something girls will do even when you don't think they are noticing you. In fact, girls are keeping a running tabulation of EVERYTHING you do, say and wear. It's what we do. And we do it WELL.

In today's teenage population, it seems boys like wearing ragged jeans, which aren't always a bad thing unless they are bagging off the butt or worse, secured with a belt beneath the butt. Shirts tucked in??? What is that all about? Boys tend to wear t-shirts that are too big, too long and often with all sorts of *junk* printed on them. Some are alright, while others are downright offensive. Their hair doesn't seem to receive much attention either, other than perhaps a wash job. I've seen guys with more hair than girls, flashback to the 70's, and it isn't pretty. Split ends, rat's nest", oily, frizzy - you name it because it seems anything goes these   days.

Taking pride in yourself and the way you appear to others speaks volumes about who you are. In fact research has been conducted and evidence found to suggest that what you wear does make a difference in how you influence the world around you. By appearing frumpy, you exude laziness, a "don't care" attitude, even an aura of "slob" to some observers. Is this really the image you want to be sending to the cute little cheerleader, the girl in drama club or the "cutie" on the volleyball team that you've had your eye on? I should hope not. In fact, you need to consider the fact that if you want her to "look back" you might want to "look better!"

So having shared with you the *female* mind and how we actually "dress you" when we're summing you up, here are a few fashion tips that you should consider BEFORE walking out the door.

- Show that you actually care & try in the morning. Begin with simple hygiene. BRUSH & FLOSS your teeth. Nothing will chase a girl off faster. Bad breath is a really BAD reflection of YOU and pretty much sums it up that you are just plain lazy. Even if you're in a hurry, this shouldn't be left off the list of "basics". Do something to your hair other than towel drying it unless you are one of the few that are lucky enough to be able to towel dry and go. (Occasionally get a haircut to trim off the dry ends, or even provide shape to your hair reflecting a style other than "anything goes".) Image is everything to teenage girls. What's on the inside matters too, but in order for her to find that out she needs and will want to be able to approach you. Wear deodorant!!! Why would you even consider walking out the door without it? Taking a shower in cologne sends the message that you were too lazy to shower and therefore you're covering your "body odor" with fragrance. Less is more. Enough said. If you have acne, as many teenagers do, consider a facial hygiene program that will help dry up and eliminate pimples. You might even consider washing mid-day at school if your situation is severe. To many girls, this can be a major turn-off. Do something to allow you to be seen and not the "bumps" all over your face. And this doesn't mean that if you have pimples, you'll go unnoticed or be ignored by the girls. Try focusing on other areas such as your wardrobe and style.

- **Dress for success**. Try to dress like you mean it. In other words, know who you are and what you like and dress accordingly. It doesn't matter  if you are punk, rock, preppy, jock, hip-hop or whatever other fashion trend you choose to emulate. Dress like you mean it but don't mean too many things. You may like many different styles, just don't try to wear them simultaneously as this will send the message that you're really confused. *Dressing fashionably* in a girl's eyes does not mean that your shoes have to match your belt. What it does mean is that you made an effort to look *put together*. You might have ironed your button down shirt to remove the wrinkles, or perhaps you coordinated your colors better than usual (no more burgundy with brown), maybe you decided to layer or accessorize. Believe it or not, it's the little things that will get you noticed and make a difference in your fashion savvy image to others. There is something to be said about the lyric of ZZ Top's song, *Everybody's Crazy About a Sharp Dressed Man*. The lyrics are true!

- **Buy quality clothes** (classic in nature) and take good care of them. Unless you are growing like a beanstalk, you should be able to get several months out of your clothes without them appearing torn and tattered. Washing them according to the care instructions will preserve not just the color but the shape and fabric of your clothes. If you focus on "classics" you can update your wardrobe by adding a few trendy items and accessories without breaking the bank.

- **Colors are important** when choosing clothes. Choose colors that both compliment and contrast. Colors that compliment would be shades that are similar and will provide you a more subtle look like blue and green or khaki and gray. Colors that contrast will "play off" each other. For example, black and white or denim and red. You might also consider colors that will compliment you. If you're redheaded, a red turtleneck shirt might not be the way to go. Choose colors that will enhance your skin tones, eye color and hair color. It's that important.

- **Accessorize.** Okay, I know I said that girls don't really expect your shoes and belt to match, but it doesn't hurt and some girls do look at this in a guy's ensemble. If you're wearing tennis shoes and a belt, you'll have to work it out the best way possible. Necklaces are also a good look and can be found to coordinate with any style you choose. Don't rule out your St. Christopher, Cross or other jewelry representative of your beliefs. Remember, you should dress to reflect "WHO" you are and this includes accessories. Accessories include hats - but keep them to a minimum. If you're constantly sporting a cap of some type, girls don't really know what you're sporting under the cap. Caps are cool - just in moderation. Finally, cool shades can say a lot about your fashion sense. But, for just as fashionable as they can make you appear, they can also make you look like a real chump. Wear them when it's appropriate. IN class, the lunchroom, or gym...not so much.

- **Experiment with fashion** and different styles as there are so many to choose from. But remember, make sure the "style" fits *who* you are inside. If you're a skateboarder, showing up in cowboy boots, jeans and a cowboy hat may be a little out there. Sure, the outfit might look great - just not great on you. Be yourself. Try Urban; Prep; Sophisticated; Artsy; Punk; Surfer; Retro; and Modern. Try to mix different looks but keep it real.

- When choosing your clothes, especially your pants, you'll want to really **consider the fit** of the pants - especially denim. STAY AWAY from jeans that are tapered (fitted at the ankle) as this should be an absolute NO! Girls like pants that are slightly loose-fitted in the leg with a bit of a boot-cut ankle. These are usually always flattering. Girls like your pants to fit you - not bag off, and certainly not to fit tighter than their own.

It is always good to know what things to "stay away" from when choosing your wardrobe and the fashion personality that reflects who you are. As a rule of thumb, avoid the following:

- **Dressing baggy from head-to-toe**...not a fashion statement that you'll want to burden yourself with. What are you carrying beneath all of that - Twinkies? Guys don't like girls in "tent dresses" and guys dressing baggy are the equivalent of that fashion "No No". Wearing t-shirts that hang almost to your knees or even below your butt make your legs look three inches long. What's that about? And wide-legged jeans make you look nothing more than WIDE - not athletic, muscular, or physically fit. Just wide.

- **DON'T wear athletic socks** with non-athletic shoes - get the point? This fashion statement screams *HELP ME* and *I'M A NERD*. Wear the proper sock or NONE AT ALL with the proper shoe. Just in case you didn't get this one...Athletic socks don't work with loafers, oxfords, leather boots, and most of all leather sandals. NEVER, EVER, EVER (unless you're a sixty-five year old retiree from Jersey living in Miami Beach)!!!

So guys, I hope that these simple tips will help you realize "What Girls Want" when looking to establish the new you. It's not rocket science, its pure chemistry.

For tips on dressing smarter, and looking smarter in your "duds", check out fashion(s) that you see on TV, movies, fashion magazines or even when walking through department stores. Go online and check out "what" and "how" some of your favorite actors dress. You can even ask your mom. Believe it or not, she was once a teenager and had an eye for "guy" fashion and I'll bet she's still got it. There are countless ways to "dress for success". You just need to step outside of your comfort zone and try on something new.

For a funny video on one fashion trend you'll want to avoid, watch the attached YouTube video, Pants on the Ground at http://www.youtube.com/watch?v=P0Z2CqJ1sRM

NOTE: The advice regarding "guy" fashion was taken from various interviews and comments made by teenage girls.

CHAPTER TWENTY-ONE

WHAT BEGINS WITH THE LETTER "U"?

Understanding Why Children Stutter-Stammer When Speaking

Of late, there has been a lot of attention given to the speech impediment known as stuttering or stammering, thanks to the release of the movie, *The King's Speech* starring Colin Firth. Stuttering or stammering has been around for a very long time and for the most part, unless we are directly affected, we've paid it very little attention. Sadly, many individuals are affected by this disorder which makes it difficult to do even the most basic thing in life which is to communicate verbally with others! Due to the knowledge that I've now obtained on the subject, I'm sharing it with you, my readers, so that you'll also be aware of the disability and perhaps develop a true sensitivity to individuals who suffer with it.

In the movie, *The Kings Speech*, the son of King George (mother of Queen Elizabeth) is unable to speak without a significant stutter. It results in his inability to function with the respect and admiration of those with whom he is required to engage in conversation. In fact, he is ridiculed, mocked and often disregarded as individuals consider him weak minded due to the impediment. Individuals who suffer from speech disorders such as stammering and stuttering are clearly misunderstood so let's review what stuttering is, the signs and symptoms of stuttering, diagnosis, and what can be done to reduce or eliminate it from one's speech patterns.

What is Stuttering? (Also known as stammering):

Stuttering is a speech impediment which often results when there are too many disruptions in the production of speech sounds. For instance, I'm sure you've heard individuals who, when speaking, utilize an overabundance of "uh's, um's and oh's". These are referred to as disfluencies (specifically interjections) in speech production and are quite common - even by individuals who aren't considered to have a speech production disorder. The problem exists when there are too many disfluencies present impeding an individual's ability to communicate effectively.

Stuttering usually becomes noticeable during childhood and will often last throughout one's lifetime. Parents aren't usually aware of speech production difficulties until their children begin speaking in sentences of more than a few words at a time. Stuttering will often invade many activities in a person's life, whether it is when talking on the telephone, in front of large groups or perhaps when in an environment that brings with it some level of discomfort or stress to the individual. In some cases, it is an issue across the board meaning that they struggle with communication at home, school, work and/or social situations. As a result, many of these individuals will limit their participation in basic activities to avoid having to communicate with others. Why? They are often embarrassed or fear the reactions of others with whom they are attempting to communicate. Some stutterers may attempt to camouflage their speech difficulties by stopping mid-way in a sentence and pretending to have forgotten their train of thought; others will rearrange the words in a sentence in order to get the words out perhaps in an unusual order while others may decline speaking at all. Either way, it is truly a tragedy for those who have disengaged themselves from others in order to eliminate the need for communication.

Here are a few statistics that go along with stuttering:

- Stuttering will often appear between the ages of 2-1/2 and 4 years of age. Although infrequent, stuttering can develop during elementary school.
- Stuttering is more common in males than females and in fact, it is estimated that boys are three to four times more likely to stutter.
- Approximately 75% of preschoolers who may develop a stutter will also stop.

Signs and Symptoms of Stuttering:

As outlined below, stuttering or stammering is a disruption of speech making it often difficult for others to follow the pattern of speech and the information being relayed. But there is more to stuttering than one might realize. Stuttered speech also includes increased repetition of words or parts of words, such as when an individual may state, "*I, I, I, I, I* want a c-c-c-cookie" or as in prolongations of speech sounds such as in the example c-c-c-ookie. Finally, you may notice part-word repetition which would be something like "*Wh-Wh-Wh-What time is it?*"

Individuals that stutter may seem to be out-of-breath and incredibly tense when attempting to communicate with others. There are many reasons for these mannerisms and understanding them will help us be more compassionate toward the individual. Some stutterers will actually appear to get the words "stuck" on their tongues without being able to utter a sound. This is described by many stutterers as the words being *blocked* in their throat. They know "what" they want to say, it just won't come out without some form of delay in their speech pattern. Often, an interjection may be used to help "produce" the sound(s) that the individual is attempting to make and will frequently is in the form of an "um", "like" or some other word or sound used to allow the speech to flow freely. Again, everyone struggles to get the words out from time to time, stutterers find it difficult ALL of the time.

Diagnosing a Stutter:

It is not always to identify all of the signs and symptoms of a stutter. The repetitive sounds, prolongations of speech and interjections are easily observed by those listening to the individual who struggles to get the words out but there are unobserved difficulties as well. As a result, consulting with a certified speech-language pathologist (SLP) is the best course of action to take.

During the evaluation, the SLP will observe and note the following:

- The number and type of speech disruptions/disfluencies a person produces within a specified period of time and in various situations too.
- How the individual reacts to and copes with the disfluencies produced.
- Speech Rate.
- Language Skills.
- Severity of the symptoms identified and how it impacts their daily lives.

Information will also be obtained regarding particular circumstances or factors that may lead to or result in the stuttering becoming worse, for instance, teasing, mocking, or perhaps being tired, etc...Additionally, the SLP will want a history of the disfluencies including the age when the symptoms were first discovered, the current age of the patient and information about family members who may exhibit stuttering as well.

After all of the information is assessed, reviewed and analyzed, the SLP will be able to determine whether a fluency disorder exists and the extent to which it has affected the individual's ability to communicate with others and participate in life's daily activities.

Although the diagnosis is pretty consistent between adults and children, there are additional factors that will be considered when diagnosing young children. First and foremost the SLP will want to evaluate to determine whether there is a likelihood that the stuttering will continue throughout the child's lifetime or whether it is likely that it may subside with time. The evaluation will include multiple tests, observations and interviews that will be used to determine the risk of continued stuttering.

Included in these additional tests will be:

- Family history - did the father, grandmother or mother of the child struggle with stuttering as a child, adult, etc....
- Timeline - when did the stuttering begin and how long has it occurred to date; 1 - 3 months; 4 - 6 months; 6 months or more.
- Other speech and/or language disorders;
- Anxiety/Fear as expressed by the child or his/her family regarding stuttering.

Unfortunately, there is no isolated factor or single-predicator that will determine or help a SLP identify the likelihood of the child's stuttering continuance. The combination of all of the information obtained will help to determine the best treatment and course of action to be taken at this point in time to help reduce eliminate or provide successful intervention(s) for the child and/or adult.

Treatments for Calming a Stutter:

Treating a stutter focuses more behavioral triggers than medical reasons as there isn't a medicine that will reduce or eliminate a stutter. Treatment will focus on skills and techniques to help the individual manage their disorder and improve their ability to communicate orally. For example, the SLP may teach the individual to control his/her breathing. Calming breaths will help the individual through providing a sense of relaxation by reducing anxiety often exhibited when speaking. They will also learn how to monitor and control the speed at which they speak. By slowing speech rates and patterns they will often be able to speak with less disfluency in their sentences. Additionally, they will be instructed and observed as they learn to put together fewer words which enable them to produce smoother flow of the words they are attempting to elicit. Treatment will take time and patience. It may be necessary for the individual to seek treatment on a daily, weekly or monthly basis and follow-up will be critical for continued successes.

It is important to realize that people who stutter are already critically aware of their inability to express themselves to others without feelings of tension or anxiousness. But did you know that there are things that individuals who are listening to people that stutter will often do which makes them more painfully aware than ever of their problem? For instance, completing sentences or filling in the blanks results in the speech becoming more disfluent as they become aware of one's impatience for them to complete their statement; interrupting their train of thought is also something to be avoided as it is difficult enough for them to complete a sentence when they're able to focus on what they want to say. Individuals who stutter want to be treated like anyone else - with the same level of respect and consideration. Please allow them the time to generate what they desire to communicate and then listen patiently. Avoid making statements such as, "take a deep breath", "calm down" or "take your time" as this too makes it more difficult for them to focus and concentrate as it results in more frustration and anxiety often resulting in their inability to complete their statement without more stuttering.

Individuals who stutter will develop their own strategies along with those learned from SLP's to enable themselves to communicate at a level that they feel more comfortable and confident in doing. It is helpful, should you find yourself needing to communicate regularly with an individual who struggles with stuttering, to simply ask the individual how they would like you (the listener) to respond when communicating. Letting the individual know that you are interested in "WHAT" they have to say and not "HOW" they say it will certainly reduce their level of anxiety, tension and awkwardness. For example, "I notice that you stutter." "I don't want you to feel uncomfortable when interacting with me so please tell me how you'd like me to respond when and/if you stutter." This statement should be made in a non-condescending manner providing the individual the confidence and sincerity necessary to engage in a conversation with you given that he/she will stumble upon certain words.

Although the exact cause of stuttering is unknown, studies suggest that an individual's genetics may play a significant role. It may perhaps be the individual inherited traits that have resulted in a stutter due to an impairment of one being able to produce sentences fluently in part due to an inability to control various muscle movements required. Whatever the underlying reason, it is something that makes communication difficult for many stricken with the disorder. With this in mind, recognizing how we can help vs. how we hurt is something that each of us can do to reduce the frustration, embarrassment and anxiety that goes hand-in-hand with speech production issues.

I encourage you, if you've not already, to watch the movie, *The King's Speech*. It is truly a touching movie and allows viewers to recognize the emotional, social and interpersonal difficulties experienced by individuals who suffer with stuttering/stammering. Although a movie, it provides an excellent depiction of stuttering and how individuals have suffered for many years.

CHAPTER TWENTY-TWO

WHAT BEGINS WITH THE LETTER "V"?

Vacationing with Kids

Traveling with kids, if you've ever done it, will either result in a huge *Cheshire Cat* grin or make you cringe at the very thought of it. Whether the memory is of traveling with your own children, someone else's children, or be a frightful memory of your own travels as a child, I'm pretty sure you've had an experience and have an opinion on the topic.

Traveling with children doesn't have to be a nightmare. In fact, if you plan properly taking the necessary steps to ensure that your children are occupied or engaged in non-life threatening activities, you've eliminated 95% of the stresses typically associated with taking that long distance vacation.

I remember my travels as a child all too well. I traveled along with my parents and two of my sisters from Maryland to California. We were blessed with beautiful weather and gorgeous scenery which all changed as we dealt with a dreadfully carsick sister. Oh yes, for nearly three hours she threw up into the floorboard, a cup or anything else my parents could come up with along the way. Apparently this was before the invention of plastic bags that you can get at any grocery store, convenience or department store. Oh what joyful memories. Years passed and I traveled from Florida to Georgia with the same sister, her two sons and my two sons. The weather was terrible, a rainy day, freezing cold temperatures and her screaming toddler who belted out the loudest screams five out of the eight hours (on which was normally a four and a half hour) trip while the other of her children projectile vomited across my car. Ugh....

You can bet that after experiences like these, whenever I prepare for a trip, I do my homework. I prepare, plan some more and double-check my plans to ensure that I never relive or revisit my past traveling nightmares.

There are many items available that make traveling with kids much less frustrating and more enjoyable for everyone involved. And these items/tips aren't just for kids. In fact, some of the most important tips I'm about to present to you are for "Parents only". So, grab a notepad or transcribe into your cellphone, because you don't want to miss a single tip.

First and foremost, let's begin with Tips for Parents. After all, unless I'm mistaken, you're probably the person(s) responsible for planning the vacation, trip or adventure. So, it makes sense to begin with you. Trust me, you can learn from my inexperience and mistakes.

Travel Tips for Adults Only

1. *Where are you going?* I mean.....WHERE are you going? Parents, buy a map or an Atlas, purchase an automotive navigation system or download the application to your cell phone. This will help ensure that you KNOW where you're going. There is nothing worse than adding an extra hour or two or four to your trip because YOU GOT LOST! If you think the kids aren't going to make you pay dearly - guess again. I've utilized the hi-tech navigation system(s) on past travels. It doesn't hurt to have a map anyway because more times than not, you're going to venture into an area that your navigation system won't have maps available sending you on a wild goose chase to your destination. Do your homework! Call ahead if you must and get specific directions. But wait! Calling ahead won't always guarantee your timely arrival. In fact, following directions like "you'll go about 4 miles (should have been 1 mile) until you see the falling down barn on your left, pass it and drive until you see the hay field, etc..." You get the point. Verify your driving directions using multiple sources to avoid this travel nightmare.

2. *How long will it take to get there?* This is debatable. If you're told that the trip, according to MapQuest, Google Maps and your navigation system, is estimated to take four hours, you'll probably need to add another one and a half or more hours to the calculation. Interestingly enough, these wonderful tools NEVER take into account a) traffic accidents; b) traffic jams, congestion or flow; c) road construction; d) potty breaks; or e) food stops, etc... Yes, you must account for each of these events if you want to travel with fewer hitches. In fact, it's almost like the travel tools we utilize are providing us travel times based on traveling via Germany's Autobahn. It is always a wise idea to check in advance and plan your travel time accordingly for items a - e above. If not, instead of the "suggested" travel time of

two and a half hours from Fayetteville, GA (south of Atlanta) to Dahlonega, GA (north of Atlanta) it could take four hours.

3. *Accommodations*!!! Never, ever, ever travel with children WITHOUT having your evening accommodations arranged in advance. TRUST ME on this one. Who knew that every small town within an hour of Disney World would be hosting some sort of "festival" on the very weekend we set off for a mini-vacation? Oh yes, it's true. We stopped at every exit attempting to find a place to rest our weary bodies. And, every place we stopped was filled to capacity. We even asked the desk clerks to check with other hotel chains for a place that we could spend the night. We found one and it was scarier than "Bates Motel". Case and point - be prepared.

Okay, now that we've addressed the Adults only section of traveling with kids, let's focus on the preparedness elements that revolve around the children. I know you'll be all too familiar with the first tip, so PLEASE don't think that just because you tell them too, they will.

Travel Tips for Parents Planning for Children

1. Make certain that you instruct and verify (listen through the door if you must) that your children go to the bathroom AND USE IT!!! If you don't you'll be stopping thirty minutes down the road.

2. Provide your children (and your husband) a snack, meal or something substantial forty-five minutes prior to walking out the door. Hopefully this will save you the hassle, time lost and money spent driving through or eating at a restaurant.

3. This is the MOST important step in preserving your sanity so again, read carefully. Depending upon the ages of your children, make lists of suggested entertainment items for them to bring along for the ride. Then, supervise to ensure that each of the items on the list, along with batteries, electric cords, chargers, adapters, and whatever else their little heart's desire, make it into the small "carry on" bag that will accompany them into the vehicle. If you have toddlers or small children, you will want to pack a bag for them with items that you deem appropriate for travel. Keep in mind, items with small pieces will lead to trouble because your child will undoubtedly drop them between the cracks in the seat, on the floor, or even between the luggage and coolers packed neatly behind the seats.

Now that we've established a method for insuring that *sanity saving entertainment items* is packed, let's identify the "Top Ten Items that Entertain when Traveling with Children".

1. If your car is not equipped with a build-in one, a portable DVD Player AND MOVIES - for each age group traveling. This item alone will provide hours of fun entertainment so "Are We There Yet?" will be replaced with the sound of laughter.

2. Snacks, Snacks & More Snacks. It is always wise when traveling with children to pack drinks (juice boxes are great) along with plenty of water, and fun as well as healthy snacks. **Note**: Keep them centrally located where you can get to them easily and I'd recommend a medium sized collapsible cooler. Good suggestions are small bags of popcorn or trail mix; perhaps fruit (either individually packed or pre-washed fruit. **NOTE #2**: Apple slices can be dipped into Sprite prior to packing to prevent them from turning brown. Fruit roll ups; crackers (cheese, peanut butter, etc...); individual packs of cereal(s); string cheese; sandwiches; veggies; something sweet always delights the kids like cookies, candy bars or even pre-packaged pudding or applesauce (don't forget the spoons). Remember, if traveling with a toddler or young child, some snacks can present choking hazards which can prove dangerous while on the road. Pack smart.

3. Older children love to have their music, so IPod or other music devices, cell phones, headphones, etc....are a good thing to pack. This is where charging devices are important.

4. Handheld games will ALWAYS save the day - as long as they are charged, can be charged, and include headphones so as not to drive you or someone else in the car crazy with the sounds some of the games repeatedly make.

5. Disposable cameras (labeled with each child's name) are a lot of fun for children when traveling. It's always interesting to see what they found photo-worthy upon returning from the trip.

6. A book, magazine or something of interest to read. When all else fails, these don't require batteries or electricity.

7. A journal or something to record the events of the trip. Fun & easy.

8. A deck of cards. There are plenty of card games that can be played while traveling. For example, *Go Fish*, *Crazy Eights*, *Old Maid*, and *Uno*.

9. **Magnetic games** were created, I believe, just for traveling with children. A few that come to mind are *Scrabble, Tic Tac Toe, Bingo, Battleship, Chess, Checkers, Sorry - Fun on the Run,* and *Alphabet letters,* numbers or colorful cubes for younger travelers.

10. Coloring books with crayons, puzzles, felt boards with felt figures, paper for folding or creating neat things like Origami and string which can be used for creating string figures like "Jacob's Ladder", "Kitty Whiskers" and "Cup and Saucer".

Now it is safe to say that you've become familiar with "WHERE" you are going, "HOW" to get there and "HOW LONG" it should take based on the factors that you've evaluated in advance. You've made and verified your reservations so there will be some form of "ACCOMMODATION" awaiting your arrival. You've determined "WHAT" items to pack or have the children pack (supervised of course) to ensure everyone is occupied and happy during the trip. You've all "EATEN" something of substance and used the "POTTY" to prevent the need to stop twenty minutes down the road for either. We're almost there.

Let's review a few additional essentials to take along for the ride. We'll call them, **Just in Case** supplies. It is always wise to pack the following items placing them in an easily accessible location because you just never know when you might need them and it is far better to be prepared than not. I'm always picked on by my family about "over preparing" until something occurs and everything we need is in the **Just in Case** bag. So, here are a few items that you really should make certain you have available.

1. Cell Phone & Charger - Prepaid / Disposable
2. Emergency Roadside Assistance plan. Make certain you have your membership card and a telephone number. I. e AAA, AARP.
3. Jumper cable, car jack, and spare tire (never leave home without them).
4. **Flashlight** (with replacement batteries)
5. First Aid Kit - I always include prescription medications, over-the-counter medicines like Ibuprofen, Tylenol, Eye Drops, Ear Drops, Bactine, Neosporin, etc...
6. Blanket(s)
7. Gallon of Water (in case the vehicle overheats)
8. Emergency Cash or Cash Card.

Okay, we're almost there. Allow me a few additional suggestions that will make traveling easier for you and the entire family.

1. Always fill the car with fuel & pack the car the night before; or if you are inclined to follow Tip #3, the morning of the day you plan to travel. It is always a good idea to ensure that children and adults take their own pillow. Younger children also like to take along their favorite stuffed animal and/or blankets. Whatever keeps them comfortable will keep them happy.

2. Plan on leaving early in the morning. Traffic is light, kids are groggy and will more than likely go back to sleep allowing you several hours without stopping. If you plan ahead, you can usually make your first stop a "breakfast" stop.

3. Begin your trip in the early evening. This works best for me although it isn't for everyone. You must be certain that the driver(s) are able to remain alert and awake during the wee hours. Traveling at night ensures that the children will sleep for a major portion of the trip. For example, begin your trip at 6:30 p.m. (after rush hour). Plan your first stop around dinner time, eat and let the kids run around outside/inside (depending on the venue you've elected to visit) wearing themselves out. This should ensure a peaceful trip.

SPECIAL NOTE: For moms traveling alone with children, stop only to go to the bathroom at busy gas stations or restaurants where there are lots of people and the area well lighted. **LOCK** your doors whenever you exit the vehicle and take everyone with you when you go to the bathroom and/or restaurant. **NEVER** leave a child alone or with other children in an automobile. If possible, ALWAYS stop at gas stations where you can pay at the pump via credit card and choose a pump that is in full view of the attendant still remembering to lock the vehicle doors.

These tips have been tried and tested. By following the suggestions I've presented, you and your family should be on your way to Happy Travels. Oh yes, and remember, ALWAYS take plastic bags for the child that will inevitably become carsick.

CHAPTER TWENTY-THREE

WHAT BEGINS WITH THE LETTER "W"?

Working Moms (Stay-At-Home Moms)

Before giving birth to my first son, I had every intention of going back to work as an elementary school teacher. Once I held my son in my arms for the first time and looked into his precious little face, I realized that everything I once felt about being a working mom changed in that instant. Now this is not to say that just because I decided that

becoming a "stay-at-home" mom was even a remote possibility. But nevertheless, I decided that this was what I wanted more than anything. The best I could hope for was a few months at home before it would become necessary for me to return to the classroom.

Not every "mom to be" wants to remain home as a full time mom or vice versa. And no matter one's opinion on the topic, for some it is quite likely to change after the bundle of joy arrives. For me, finding a career, hobby or job opportunity that would allow me to remain at home with my new baby became a priority. Believe me, it was not an easy topic to introduce to my husband but one, nonetheless, that I took very seriously. Eliminating or even reducing the household income when the expenses of a new child are incurred is a tremendous consideration for many new families.

I began researching every opportunity that I could find, specifically jobs that included "work from home" in their advertising. I quickly found out that fancy advertising found in magazines, radio and television led me down a costly path. I immediately discovered that the saying, "If it sounds too good to be true it probably is" couldn't have been more true. I made the decision, after falling for one scam too many, that I needed to focus on my capabilities and determine what I could realistically do to earn a supplemental income allowing me both flexibility and freedom to remain home with my son.

After weighing many options, I discovered that watching another child in my home was the most cost effective solution. I needed very little equipment in addition to what I already owned and the arrangement allowed me to remain home and enjoy raising and interacting with my son. It provided my "only" child the opportunity to grow socially as well since he was able to interact with another child his age. We earned a nice income doing something I wanted to do anyway AND I was able to use my background in education to make it work. When my son turned three, I decided that expanding our horizons was a good idea and I enrolled him in a local preschool  where I also obtained employment as a Pre-Kindergarten teacher. This allowed both of us to spread our wings and benefit not only financially but emotionally and socially as well. I was able to do this while pregnant with my second child.

There are many opportunities out there for moms needing to bring in an income but not at the expense of missing those irreplaceable infant and toddler years and just as many for moms feeling the need to remain "available" indefinitely. All you have to do is focus on your strengths and abilities and do a little research within your community to determine "what" is available or what you can offer. By inquiring with individuals in my own community, I found many opportunities that were perfect for me.

Upon the birth of my second son, and desiring to remain home with him, I utilized my former contacts and found that a local movie production studio rented/leased rooms or entire homes while filming movies in our area. Owning an 1830's Victorian home which we'd recently renovated, I was able to lease (3) bedrooms for several months at a time bringing in a wonderful income. This job opportunity might not be an option for you, but what it does reflect is my ability and desire to utilize what I had available in order to remain home with my children.

In my inner circle of friends alone, desiring to remain home with their children, were part-time bank tellers and office receptionists, substitute teachers, sales associates at specialty stores, private childcare providers, mom's that job-shared or worked from home via computer, mom's that cleaned houses for others of even prepared meals for working professionals. Some mom's provided transportation for other working mom's children (Mom's Taxi) and some assembled products at home for local companies. There were tutors, personal trainers and graphic designers. Other friends pulled specifically from their craft and hobby experiences designing, creating and selling floral arrangements; seamstresses who sewed exclusively for local cheerleading squads providing uniform alterations; and moms who used their skills in photography to take photos of sporting events at schools and selling them on CD to proud parents. There were so many amazing opportunities for moms seeking careers that would allow them a lifestyle at home that provided them a chance to be available to their child they just had to determine what worked for them.

If none of these jobs appeal to you, there are other opportunities that may be just right for you. There are many companies that allow moms to work from home but you have to be selective in choosing them. If you'd like additional information on an opportunity that I personally have experience, you can visit my website www.wahunation.com or send a message to agreenerlife2016@gmail.com and I'll reply with the resource.

Now that my children are in young adults with one a Nuclear Engineer in the U.S. Navy and one in college, I still want to be available for them just the same as I have been since the day they were born. Often times, parents feel that because their children are grown or perhaps are mature enough, if only in their minds, that it is alright to allow them to come home after school and take care of themselves. Or perhaps they simply don't worry quite as much about being available as their children are perfectly capable of self-management. There is a great deal of research out there on the pros and cons of both....but that's another topic in another book.

Be creative. The sky is literally the limit and you can achieve your ultimate goal if you take the time to "make a list" of your skills, hobbies, interests and anything that you can realistically do for others, as well as a list of individuals or contacts with whom you can discuss the possibilities. You'd be surprised at just how many opportunities you'll find or create and which can provide a significant income to make your dreams of remaining home with your children a reality.

CHAPTER TWENTY-FOUR

WHAT BEGINS WITH THE LETTER "X"?

Handling Extreme Personalities in Children

Have you ever seen a child who always seems to push the proverbial envelope and thought to yourself, "Whew, thank goodness he/she isn't mine"? Over the years as an elementary school teacher and then as a mother of two amazing boys I've seen my share of children with extreme personalities and have thanked the good Lord above that he/she wasn't my challenge. Not because they were less deserving of love or weren't as easy to love, but because I felt that their "on-the-go" risky, hurtful behavior was a bit more than I could handle as a mom without losing my mind. Well, those children are out there and they typically grow up to be that same risk-taker they were as a child just in a larger frame – complete with physical and emotional scars, and all of their limbs if they're lucky. What do you do if you have one of these cowboys/cowgirls running around your home? Breathe deeply and develop strategies that will help rein him/her in and hopefully reduce the number of risky behaviors that may lead to injury, death, or unfulfilled potential.

When my children were young we had a neighbor who was always pushing the envelope in terms of activities that weren't considered safe by many or within the limits many parents establish for their children. This child was out of control by every standard that I deemed acceptable and had not only hurt himself on many occasions but influenced or "bullied" many other children in the neighborhood to act inappropriately as well leading to some form of harm or activity that was illegal. Consequently, my children were forbidden from playing with him as he was unable or unwilling to follow the rules established and **always** set a bad example for them and the other children in the neighborhood. Luckily for me and my children, I was able to explain to my sons that as a result of his choices, ill-behavior, actions, attitude and unwillingness to follow the established rules; they would have to excuse themselves whenever he came around.

This child seemed to have parents who'd allow him to do whatever he wanted, whenever, without any form of accountability or consequence for his actions and choices. Sound extreme? Trust me when I say that this child lacked the supervision or parental guidance necessary to keep him on the right track and lacked any type of self-regulatory control within him to help govern his words and actions. The child was a danger to himself and to others.

As most parents recognize and understand, children are precious and need adult supervision, parameters and guidance to help control or at least curb their behaviors. Much like that of a family pet who must be taught not to destroy the furniture or shoes, eat things that can harm him or how to behave when in the presence of people. Unfortunately for this child, he never received any of the necessary parental interventions needed to help rein him in or at the least provide the much-needed parameters within which the child could operate. The child was alienated by most children who knew him which only led to more acting out and destructive behaviors.

I am not a doctor but what I observed was that the child exhibited the types of behaviors often associated with ADHD, Oppositional Defiant Disorder and Conduct Disorder as many of these overlap in child behaviors. As an adult, his behaviors would be classified as Antisocial Personality Disorder. For those of you who are aware of these types of behavior, you know the importance of seeking assistance from a medical professional to help learn strategies necessary when dealing with extreme personality types. For those of you who may be unfamiliar with extreme personalities often referred by parents as a "wild child" type of personality, you'll want to become educated and begin establishing rules, consequences, and parameters immediately.

Traits Associated with Extreme Personalities:

- Disregard for the rights of other people manifesting itself as hostility and/or aggression. This individual is proficient at deceit and manipulation.
- Individuals who hurt or torment animals and/or people – often classified or considered to be a bully.
- These children often use intimidation tactics when engaging with others.
- Children who have a reckless disregard for property, i.e. setting fires.
- Often engage in deceit, theft, and other serious infractions of standard rules of conduct.

In addition to the qualities and characteristics referenced above, these children may:

- Find themselves in dangerous and/or risky situations.

- Act on impulse urges without considering the consequences of their actions.
- Typically do not experience real or genuine remorse for the harm they cause others (unless they feign remorse because it lends itself to their best interest, i.e. when in court before a judge).
- They take little or no responsibility for their actions and often blame their victims or others for their actions and consequently their fate.

Individuals who demonstrate these types of behavioral abnormalities will often struggle with employment, accidents of all sorts, and legal difficulties which often lead to incarceration. These individuals and the aggressive features known to be associated with this particular personality disorder wreak havoc on society.

What Intervention Steps are Necessary?

When living with a child who demonstrates the behaviors mentioned above, you're going to have your hands full. It is wise to know what types of parenting tools and strategies are necessary to help manage and control these behaviors preventing them from getting out of control. I'll refer to them as *Practical Tools and Interventions* necessary for the management of patients or individuals with Conduct Disorder.

- Assess the severity of the disorder which may require a medical professional/counselor.
- Determine if there is any form of substance abuse occurring that you aren't currently aware (marijuana, pharmaceutical drug abuse, alcohol, huffing, or other hallucinogenic drugs) and treat/tackle/manage this first.
- Structure activities that implement consistent behavior parameters.
- Establish a system to monitor your child's activities (who they are fraternizing with and where they are at all times). If this isn't eyes on your child specifically, it should include frequent and regular telephone contact, text(s) between parent and child or even some sort of physical whereabouts monitoring, i.e. location device or service via cellphone service provider.
- Create a curfew that MUST be adhered too along with consequences that will result no matter what the circumstance.

- Determine activities that will be structured and supervised (sports, scouting, etc.…) and register your child to participate.
- Practice clear and concise parental communication techniques with your child.
- Establish appropriate rewards for desirable practiced behaviors.
- Create and communicate realistic consequences for noncompliance of appropriate behaviors.
- Establish a positive and supportive emotional climate by setting aside a minimum of 15 minutes per day for parent and child to play and engage together (i.e. playing catch, drawing, coloring, reading or simply talking). This structured time reinforces contact between parent and child.
- If necessary, discuss and implement a pharmacotherapy for children who are highly aggressive and/or lack impulse control (or both).

Conduct disorder may not be the same for all children and will vary in degrees of severity. Although there are many factors which may determine the severity of the disorder, many of the strategies listed above can and must be implemented successfully and consistently to reduce the inappropriate behaviors in most children.

Children with conduct disorder may not recognize these unappealing traits within themselves, their actions or behaviors. It is up to parents, caregivers, teachers and counselors to help children recognize these behaviors and then learn effective methods to implement to reduce and/or eliminate them altogether.

As a rule of thumb, I would exhaust all behavior modification strategies before utilizing pharmaceutical drugs to curb and/or manage impulses and behavior as it may not be worth the side-effects often associated with long term use of medications.

CHAPTER TWENTY-FIVE

WHAT BEGINS WITH THE LETTER "Y"?

Youth Summer Camps

It's nearly that time of year again when children finish their school term and embrace the summer months. While children only view the summer months with a smile and see the "free time" ahead, parents are and have been struggling with how the summer months will impact the children and family. To help alleviate this stress, I'd say parents should begin looking at summer camps and the many options that are available to children in and around their   community.

Summer camps are a wonderful opportunity for children to remain active or intellectually engaged throughout the summer months. It sure beats them sleeping until noon, followed by countless hours on the couch watching television, snacking (or in my case, eating us out of house and home), or the wasted mental capacity devoted to one form of video game or another. Add to this lack-luster schedule that many children will be left unattended and you have a recipe for potential disaster.

The Benefits of Summer Camp:

If you are a parent that is employed throughout the summer months, sending your child to a day camp or even a week long camp away from home will allow him/her to enjoy the company of other children while under the supervision of camp counselors. It will help to eliminate the need to leave him/her at home alone daily with little or nothing productive to do. Summer camps are a lot of fun for children and provide many educational and opportunities for him/her to learn something new. Summer camps are great for teaching children a new sport or even providing the time to improve at something your child could use a little extra something to get them up to par.

Camps are excellent opportunities for children to engage with other children from various backgrounds and to establish new and lasting relationships. Children enjoy the company of age-mates and really enjoy the chance to *get away* from their siblings if only for a day or two and yes, their parents too.

A Look at Summer Camps:

Summer camps are offered in many locations which can be obtained by visiting the worldwide web. Depending upon the type of camp you're looking for, of which there are literally hundreds, and the budget that you have to delegate to camp, you'll more than likely be able to find the perfect opportunity that will both please your child AND your pocketbook too!!!

Since my children were little guys, I began enrolling them in summer camps to provide them the many opportunities that were available within our small community. They attended YMCA Day Camps, Sports Camps including baseball, basketball, football, tennis, golf and wrestling; Boy Scout camp; Arts & Science camps; All about Nature camps; Equestrian; Gymnastics, Martial Arts, surf camps and even camps which were for site-seeing adventures. Each was offered during the day, some full days while others were for half-days or a combination thereof. My boys enjoyed the new experiences that they were provided and were exposed to so many wonderful opportunities that they'd have missed if they had simply remained at home during the summer months.

When it comes to camps, the sky's the limit. In fact, there are camps for Astrology; photography; oil painting or other forms of painting; sewing; woodworking; computer camps; etc....

How to Find Camps in Your Area:

First step in locating camps within your community is to contact your local school district. Many districts offer camps throughout the summer at various schools. Camps are often available for children in grades Kindergarten through the 6th or 7th grade unless they are sports camps which will continue through the 12th grade.

YMCA also offers summer camps which are open for children between Kindergarten and 6th grade (in our community)

although this may vary within your community.

Other places that you can contact for summer camps includes local churches, sports and recreation centers, Parks and Recreation offices within your community; the public library; and your local newspaper. It is also wise to check with various colleges and universities near your community as they will often host children's camps throughout the summer perfect for the little scientist, artist or athlete in your family.

Sites that you can visit online include:

- *www.kidscamps.com/residential/overnight camp.html*
- *www.mysummercamps.com/*
- *www.kidscamps.com/*
- *www.internaldrive.com/*
- *www.acacamps.org/*
- *www.skyhawks.com/*
- *www.educationunlimited.com/*
- *www.summer-daycamps.com/*

These are but a few of the resources available. By typing in summer camps or summer camps for children in your search engine you will be taken to sites that are available for viewing which will provide plenty of information on things your child can do over the summer instead of remaining at home *alone*.

If you are unable to find a suitable camp for your children or the children within your area, perhaps starting a Summer Camp Co-op in which various adults take on the responsibility for a certain number of children on a weekly basis providing a "summer camp" experience. Keep in mind that this doesn't mean bringing a bunch of kids over to play video games or to watch television because I can assure you the outcome will more than likely be you pulling out your very last hair if it doesn't fall out on its own. What this entails is:

1. Finding other local parents that would be willing to work together to plan summer experiences for a few children. Perhaps working together collectively hosting the camps at each other's homes, church rectories or club houses within a neighborhood. Most neighborhood communities contain swimming pools, tennis

courts and some have other amenities that children will enjoy. If there is a fee involved to rent spaces, you'll want to charge a fee for hosting the camp experience.

2. Careful planning is paramount to ensure that you have enough adult supervision to monitor the children that you will be hosting. Think about your child's birthday parties (if you've hosted any at home) and how wound up children can get. Planning for one day or five days will require a pretty detailed schedule - although there should always be room for flexibility. Make certain that you don't overbook as you will find too many children difficult to manage.

3. Advertising will be necessary unless you have several close friends that you know that will be willing to spread the word to their children's friends and their parents. It is always nice to know the children that will be in and out of your home, but don't eliminate the opportunity for other children looking for quality camps and supervision from participating. Perhaps placing a flyer at your child's school; your church; or even placing an ad in the local paper.

4. Know what you'll be doing weeks in advance so that you can let parents that are interested know of any additional costs that will be needed. For example, if part of your week will include visiting the zoo, you'll want to let the parents know BEFORE you enroll them that this is part of the weekly camp plans. This will allow them to make the decision up-front whether their child will participate or not.

5. Supplies. Unless you want to become a short-order cook, you'll want to notify parents when you enroll their children that they will be responsible for providing lunch for their child. Brown bag it baby! Of course, you'll want to provide a reasonable snack or they'll be miserable if they've been playing outside or engaged in any type of physical activity. If you'll be serving any form of food and beverage, you'll want to gather medical information re: food allergies, etc....to ensure that you aren't providing something that can be harmful.

6. Gather Relevant Details. As with any form of camp, you'll want the parents to complete a form with contact information, emergency information and other relevant details as you will ultimately be responsible for their child. I also would recommend photocopies of any insurance cards in the event of emergency requiring a visit to the doctor or emergency room. Make certain that you have multiple contact numbers including places of employment and relatives or close friends.

Working together with other parents with whom you know and trust, you can earn a buck or two while providing children with a meaningful, exciting opportunity to engage with others while enjoying their summer at home (or at least away from school).

Remember, children who are actively engaged in meaningful, supervised activities are less likely to become engaged in activities that are dangerous, or that may lead them to trouble. By planning ahead, you can provide your child with a summer full of fun and exciting adventures while reducing the fears and anxieties that you might have leaving them home alone for any portion of the day. Additionally, summer camps are a great escape for the child whose parent(s) stay home or work from home to allow them to "be kids" without having to be underneath your thumb throughout the summer months. It's a good break for EVERYONE.

CHAPTER TWENTY-SIX

WHAT BEGINS WITH THE LETTER "Z"?

What Begins with the Letter "Z" Summertime Activity?

As a former teacher and mother of two very inquisitive young boys, summer activities were always critical in keeping them excited and engaged. We made the most of the summer months enjoying summer camps, vacations, and the "staycations" that kept us enjoying various activities right at home but I believed there needed to be a component that involved exercising the brain so that it didn't get rusty or require cleaning of the cobwebs come "back to school" time.

One such activity that I utilized was a game that I referred to as "What Begins with the Letter "__". This game required that each of my boys create a summer project that revolved around a letter of the alphabet that they chose themselves. I'll create an outline below so that you can see and understand for yourself what this activity is all about and how it can be included weekly for one day at a time summer vacation educational, yet fun activities.

What Begins with the Letter "Z" would include variations of the following:

- First, have your child choose a letter of the alphabet that he/she would like to investigate. Make the investigation a fun one for your child by creating props to be used, i.e. a magnifying glass, cap to be used when working on his/her project, pads, paper, pens, markers, coloring crayons, paint, clay, camera, measuring tools of all varieties, etc....plus any other props you deem necessary. This could include buckets, baskets, nets, and anything that lends itself (in your mind and that of your child's mind and imagination) into the completion of this project.

- Second, have your child list as many words as he/she can that begin with the chosen letter. For example, the letter "Z" might include: xenops (rainforest bird), zebra, zebrafish, zebra longwing butterfly, zebra swallowtail butterfly, zeppelin (not the musical group) the metal-framed motorized balloon-like airship; zero, zigzag, zinnia (the flower), zip, zipper, zither (musical instrument), zodiac signs (constellations), zodiac moth, zoo, zoologist, zooplankton, zorilla (skunk-like mammal that lives in Africa), zorro and zucchini to name a few. This list should provide some pretty exciting opportunities for artwork, research, writing, activities and discovery for you and your child to engage in together but also ample opportunities for individual study.

- Next, establish guidelines for your child that are reasonable and which you will be able to accommodate within your schedule as some of these activities may require traveling to places outside of your own backyard, i.e. garden center or store to purchase seeds to plant in a garden plot that your child has decided to create for his  very own zucchini plant; to the library or online (with parental supervision for younger children) to research the rainforest and check out books which may include information on the xenops bird that the child has identified as a letter "z" word which actually begins with the letter "x" (which could include another activity of creating a list of words that sound like they begin with the letter "z" but don't (i.e. xenops, xylophone, etc…); it may include a field trip to the local zoo (or closest one) or to a pet store to view the tropical fish; and will often include activities that you'll need to assist your child in completing (planting a garden)…I believe you understand the dynamics here.

- Establish, along with your child, a timeline or calendar so that your child knows what is expected of him/her. This activity provides an opportunity for you and your child to engage in meaningful conferencing (weekly) and one-on-one time which is critical for young children. It will teach them important life skills that they will utilize throughout their lives. It is at this time that you explain (again with input from your child) what is required of your child in order to complete this activity during summer vacation. More specifically, what the final project should include and how to incorporate the activities into a weekly schedule that will be comfortable for your child, i.e. two activities per week; one written activity per week along with one physical activity; or whatever you and your child agree upon. Creating some type of *staying focused and accountability* chart so they can keep up with their progress and accomplishments weekly will be a fun reward system for them to use. It should be something fun, reasonable and dictated by your child's age and your schedule to motivate and enhance the experience.

- Schedule a biweekly conference (over ice cream or other fun snack) to allow for input and feedback so your child isn't wandering aimlessly in the proverbial desert.

Sometimes it is helpful (especially for younger children) to have regular weekly conferences to keep your child on track and help him/her brainstorm what to do next. An example may be to help the child who has decided to plant a zucchini in his/her own garden understand what is next, for instance, he/she may require direction on what is needed to plant a garden, besides seeds and dirt? Or, a child might not think of sketching, drawing or painting his plant's growth weekly as a journal entry; or keeping a photo journal of his/her garden including insects, birds or other animals that visit it or steps he/she must take to protect their plantings. So many activities can be generated from single part of the process: measuring the height of the plant weekly to show how quickly it grows (measurement skills); photos to show how it changes (documentation skills along with photography skills); how much sunlight it requires (time telling skills); how much water it requires or receives (measurement skills); so many lessons can be learned and taken from simple activities like this one and others.

- Plan an "Unveiling" date and make it a **Grand Event** for your child to share with you, family, friends and other relatives their project from beginning to end. Send out invitations; plan a menu with your child and allow them help prepare the foods and drinks to be served. Make it something that is special so that they'll be more inclined and motivated to do it again and again, summer after summer.

Keeping children actively engaged in the learning process is as easy as creating fun activities that they can accomplish on their own or with adult engagement and supervision. They are keeping their skills sharp as they do simple projects recording and creating. With all children, any activity that involves and includes a parent or caregiver is one that is both meaningful and memorable as all children desire the attention of a loved one.

Use your summers wisely to help encourage your child learner to continue to build upon and strengthen their core skills while doing it in a way that helps facilitate the bond between children and their parents.

Enjoy your summer!

What's Next???

Stay tuned for Volume two of the series, *Children Topics from A to Z: A Guide for Tackling Tough Issues* as I'm sure it will be loaded with more information that you **won't** want to miss. Whether you are a parent, teacher, caregiver or teen who is looking for information that you need for a current or upcoming situation, you'll more than likely find it within the covers of one of these books. With well over two-hundred and fifty different topics covered, this book will make the perfect companion to your "Welcome Baby Home" supplies, your pre-existing Parenting Tips and Strategies library, or simply provide the answers to questions that you just don't feel comfortable asking others collection. There is something for everyone.

Each volume will include topics that are relevant to each age group from birth into adulthood and may include information on: *Interacting with Your Newborn* or topics or subjects such as *Attention Deficit Hyperactive Disorder*, *Meaningful Apologies and How to Make Them*, *Juvenile Diabetes*, *Relationship Building and Rescue Techniques for Parents*, *Healthy Eating for Families*, *Gluten-Free Diets*, and *Positive Discipline Techniques for Parents and Teachers*. Each book will have helpful tips and strategies that may be just what you are looking for to help raise happy, healthy babies, children and teenagers or even how to deal with situation that are difficult to tackle without additional information or advice.

Thanks for taking the time to read Volume One of the Five Part Series and stay tuned for the next volume coming to you soon.

What's Next???

Stay tuned for Volume two of the series, **Children Topics from A to Z: A Guide for Tackling Tough Issues** as I'm sure it will be loaded with more information that you won't want to miss. Whether you are a parent, teacher, caregiver or teen who is looking for information that you need for a current or upcoming situation, you'll more than likely find it within the covers of one of these books. With well over two-hundred and fifty different topics covered, this book will make the perfect companion to your "Welcome Baby Home" supplies, your pre-existing Parenting Tips and Strategies library, or simply provide the answers to questions that you just don't feel comfortable asking others collection. There is something for everyone.

Each volume will include topics that are relevant to each age group from birth into adulthood and may include information on: *Interacting with Your Newborn* or topics or subjects such as *Attention Deficit Hyperactive Disorder, Meaningful Apologies and How to Make Them, Juvenile Diabetes, Relationship Building and Rescue Techniques for Parents, Healthy Eating for Families, Gluten-Free Diets*, and *Positive Discipline Techniques for Parents and Teachers*. Each book will have helpful tips and strategies that may be just what you are looking for to help raise happy, healthy babies, children and teenagers or even how to deal with situation that are difficult to tackle without additional information or advice.

Thanks for taking the time to read Volume One of the Five Part Series and stay tuned for the next volume coming to you soon.

MEET THE AUTHOR OF CHILDREN TOPICS
FROM A TO Z

Randa Lee Roberts was born in Tallahassee, Florida on September 24, 1963 and grew up in Monticello, Florida living briefly in both Maryland and California as a young child. She attended Aucilla Christian Academy for the majority of her high school years but made a change her senior year to her parent's Alma Mater and attended Leon High School while dual-enrolled at Florida State University. After graduating from high school in 1981, she attended Tallahassee Community College from which she earned her Associate in Arts. She then attended the University of Florida earning her MA in Early Childhood Education with a BA in Elementary Education. After her first year of teaching, she returned to Florida State University and received a Specialist Degree in Educational Leadership as well as teaching in Leon County, followed by The University of West Georgia obtaining a Specialist Degree in Educational Leadership as well. She and her youngest son, a student at Kennesaw State University, currently live in Georgia while her oldest son serves in the United States Navy as a Nuclear Engineer and is stationed in Charleston, South Carolina.

Randa first knew of her desire to become an author at the young age of twelve when she first had poetry she'd written while attending middle school selected for publication. She desired to write a mystery novel and created the first draft which she is still working on. She continued to follow her dream of becoming a writer and published her first children's book, *Liver for Dinner*, in 2010. She continues her desire to write and does so in her blog, *Childrentopics.com*, where she writes articles to assist parents, teachers, caregivers and children on topics that are relevant to various issues that exist in the lives of most families in their everyday lives.

Randa released her first non-fiction book, *Surviving Cancer: A Caregiver's Guide to Survival One Step at a Time* in February 2016 receiving a Best Seller Ranking from Amazon, which details her journey as a full-time caregiver to her late-husband who was diagnosed with brain cancer while raising her two children. This book is followed by the release of; *Get the Real "Skinny" on Healthy Weight Loss: Commit to a Lifestyle*

Modification and Get Results, in March 2016, which focuses on making modifications to one's lifestyle to include diet and exercise to achieve long-term results and enhances one's overall health and wellness. With lots more to come from this up and coming author, you'll want to follow her progress and get your hands on her upcoming (5) Volume Series, ***Children Topics from A to Z: A Guide to Tackling Tough Issues*** as soon as they are released. If you're reading about the author in the back of Volume 1 of the new series, I'd say you're already in tune! Stay tuned for more….

www.ingramcontent.com/pod-product-compliance
Lightning Source LLC
Chambersburg PA
CBHW081345280526
45788CB00009B/2781